W9-ANC-876

SLAVERY

WRITTEN BY
REG GRANT

LONDON, NEW YORK,
MELBOURNE, MUNICH, AND DELHI

For Toucan Books:
Senior editor Jo Bourne
Project editor Tom Pocklington
Editor Matthew Rake
Senior designer Ralph Pitchford
Designer Nihal Yesil

For Dorling Kindersley:
Consultant James T. Campbell
Senior editor Victoria Heyworth-Dunne
Senior art editor Jacqui Swan
Managing editor Linda Esposito
Managing art editor Diane Thistlethwaite
Publishing manager Andrew Macintyre
Category publisher Laura Buller
Picture researcher Louise Thomas
Cartographer Ed Merritt
Senior production editor Viv Ridgeway
Jacket editor Mariza O'Keeffe
Jacket designer Akiko Kato
Jacket design manager Sophia Tampakopoulos-Turner
Production controller Erika Pepe
US editor Margaret Parrish

First published in the United States in 2009 by
DK Publishing
375 Hudson Street, New York, New York 10014

09 10 11 12 13 10 9 8 7 6 5 4 3 2 1
SD406 – 03/09
Copyright © 2009 Dorling Kindersley Limited, London

A catalog record for this book is available from the Library of Congress.

ISBN: 978-0-7566-5169-5

Printed by Toppan, China

Discover more at www.dk.com

SLAVERY

real people and their
stories of enslavement

WRITTEN BY
REG GRANT

THE FIGHT FOR FREEDOM

ABOLISHING SLAVERY IN THE AMERICAS

AFTERMATH OF SLAVERY

CONTENTS

*I*N THE THREE *and a half centuries after Columbus's first voyage to the Americas in 1492, more than 12 million enslaved Africans were packed into European ships and carried to the New World. The world that we live in today has been significantly shaped by the unpaid labor of these Africans and their African-American descendants.*

This unique book examines the history of slavery and its role in the making of the modern world. Like the institution of slavery itself, the book ranges from the ancient world right to the present day, which continues to be plagued by human trafficking. The book's focus is the system of African slavery that developed in the plantation colonies of the Americas—in Brazil, the Caribbean, and mainland North America, what is today the United States.

The pages that follow reveal the workings of the transatlantic slave trade, which bound the historical and economic destinies of four continents. They trace the circulation of commodities that enslaved people produced, including many—sugar, coffee, cotton, cocoa—that remain part of our daily lives today. Most importantly, they present the voices of the enslaved people themselves, describing their experiences, aspirations, and struggles for freedom in their own words.

The book you hold contains much that is ugly and sad. But it also includes stories of courage, heroism, and hope—stories that have much to teach us as we endeavor to build a better, more just world for ourselves, and those who will come after us.

FOREWORD
BY JAMES T. CAMPBELL
PROFESSOR OF HISTORY AT STANFORD UNIVERSITY

BACKGROUND TO SLAVERY

AN ENSLAVED PERSON is someone who has had his or her freedom taken away and is forced to work for a master or owner. Slavery is as old as human civilization. Until modern times, it was accepted by everyone as a fact of life. Even thinkers in Ancient Greece, who first set out the ideas of democracy and freedom, believed a free life for some was only possible through the enslavement of others. Religions such as Christianity and Islam set some limits on slavery, but at the same time accepted and supported it overall.

Rome's warrior slaves
Gladiators, shown here on a marble relief from a tomb, were prisoners or slaves specially trained in combat skills. They fought to entertain huge crowds in the arenas of Ancient Rome. Some won freedom and glory, but many more died in the contest.

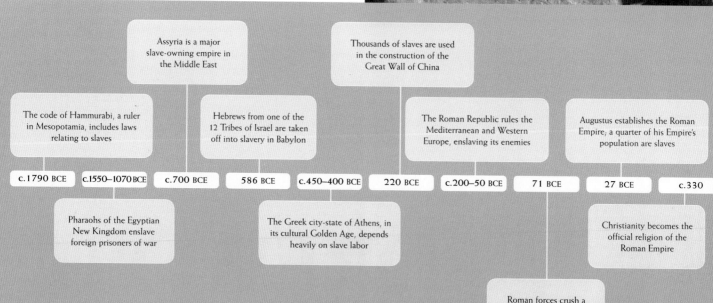

Assyria is a major slave-owning empire in the Middle East

Thousands of slaves are used in the construction of the Great Wall of China

The code of Hammurabi, a ruler in Mesopotamia, includes laws relating to slaves

Hebrews from one of the 12 Tribes of Israel are taken off into slavery in Babylon

The Roman Republic rules the Mediterranean and Western Europe, enslaving its enemies

Augustus establishes the Roman Empire; a quarter of his Empire's population are slaves

| c.1790 BCE | c.1550–1070 BCE | c.700 BCE | 586 BCE | c.450–400 BCE | 220 BCE | c.200–50 BCE | 71 BCE | 27 BCE | c.330 |

Pharaohs of the Egyptian New Kingdom enslave foreign prisoners of war

The Greek city-state of Athens, in its cultural Golden Age, depends heavily on slave labor

Christianity becomes the official religion of the Roman Empire

Roman forces crush a large-scale slave revolt led by Spartacus

Viking raiders capture and enslave people in the coastal settlements of western Europe

Spain authorizes the import of slaves from Africa into its possessions in the Americas

The prophet Muhammed founds the religion of Islam

Portuguese sailors begin trading along the west coast of Africa

At the great naval Battle of Lepanto, Muslims and Christian both use slaves to row galleys

| 622 | c.750 | c.800 | c.1300 | 1440s | 1492 | 1510 | c.1530 | 1571 | 1607 |

Enslaved Africans are first carried along slave routes across the Sahara Desert to the north

Christopher Columbus sails to the West Indies, opening the way for the European conquest of the Americas

Virginia is the first permanent English settlement in North America

The Venetians are major slave traders in the eastern Mediterranean

The Portuguese bring the first African slaves to Brazil

9

SLAVERY IN ANCIENT TIMES

THE EARLIEST CIVILIZATIONS, whether in the Middle East, East Asia, or the Americas, all had forms of slavery. People were most often enslaved after being defeated in war and carried off as prisoners. Others were enslaved as a punishment for crime or as a result of poverty. If a man could not pay his debts, he and his family might become slaves of the person they owed money to. The enslaved mostly performed hard physical labor and menial tasks no free person wanted to do.

Slave law

Some 3,800 years ago Hammurabi, the ruler of the city of Babylon in Mesopotamia (modern-day Iraq), had a set of laws carved on this tall stone, or "stele." Hammurabi's code of law mentions slaves several times. It states that anyone who is found guilty of sheltering or helping a runaway slave will be put to death.

Prisoners of war

Warfare was a major source of slaves in the ancient Middle East. Powerful states such as Egypt and Assyria, ruled by warrior emperors, used their armies to crush weaker neighboring countries and enslave their people. This Assyrian carving shows a soldier guarding two prisoners captured during an invasion of Judaea, Palestine, in 701 BCE. They were destined for slavery in Assyria.

Babylonian captivity

The Old Testament of the Bible tells how the Hebrew people were enslaved by more powerful neighboring states. They were held as slaves in Egypt and later, in 586 BCE, were carried off into captivity by the Babylonians, represented here with beards and long robes. The Babylonian captivity lasted until 538 BCE.

Jewish slave owners

Many Hebrews of the Old Testament era owned slaves themselves. Under Hebrew law foreign slaves could be held for life, but enslaved Hebrews had to be set free after a certain period of time, usually six years, or in a general "jubilee" every 50 years.

Most of the great palaces and temples of the ancient world were built by slaves.

American servitude

There were slaves in the Americas long before Europeans arrived. The Maya of Central America, for example, obtained slaves through warfare, as well as enslaving orphan children and those guilty of certain crimes. This carving from the Mayan city of Palenque in Mexico, dating from about 730 CE, is known as the Tablet of the Slaves. It shows a man of high rank holding a headdress, and a Mayan ruler sitting cross-legged on two captive men.

China's Great Wall

The original Great Wall of China was created by the Emperor Qin Shi Huang in about 220 BCE. He employed some half a million slave laborers on this mighty defensive structure, which was designed to keep warlike nomads from Central Asia out of the Chinese Empire.

ANCIENT GREECE AND ROME

EDUCATED PEOPLE IN EUROPE and the United States were once brought up to admire Ancient Greece and Rome as models of civilization. Yet these societies were based on slavery. Ancient Greek city-states such as Athens invented democracy, but their free citizens owned slaves. In Ancient Rome, slaves made up more than a quarter of the population. The Roman Empire was probably more dependent on slavery than any other ancient society.

Roman conquest
In the Roman Empire, large gangs of slaves were used to labor in mines and quarries and on farms. The Romans originally obtained slaves by war or trade. Parts of Europe, including France, Germany, and England, provided Rome with many slaves. This scene from the Emperor Trajan's Column, created to celebrate his victories in war, shows a Dacian, from modern-day Romania, taken prisoner by Roman soldiers.

There were an estimated 12 million slaves in the Roman Empire at its peak.

Spartacus fights for freedom
Occasionally, Roman slaves rebelled against their masters. The most famous uprising was led by Spartacus, a former gladiator. The rebellion was crushed by the Roman Army in 71 BCE. Spartacus died fighting and later 6,000 of his followers were executed by crucifixion. Actor Kirk Douglas played the slave leader in the 1960 movie *Spartacus*.

Slave tag
Many Roman slaves fled from ill-treatment by their owners. Runaways were pursued by professional slave-catchers as well as by the Roman authorities. When recaptured, they might be marked with an iron tag.

Gladiators in the arena
Slaves were forced to act as gladiators, staging fights with one another or with wild animals in the Colosseum and other Roman arenas. These gladiator slaves could become famous if they won many fights.

House slaves
Wealthy Romans owned household slaves who worked as servants, preparing and serving food and drink, doing the shopping, cleaning villas, and tending gardens. Educated slaves served as home tutors to Roman children and as family doctors. Household slaves generally had easier lives than slaves working in labor gangs.

VOICES
SLAVERY IN CLASSICAL GREECE AND ROME

Slavery was very much a part of life in classical society: in those days no one seems to have questioned whether or not it should exist. Philosophers pondered its place in society—but never its rights and wrongs. As for the slaves, they had to pursue their happiness as best they could.

"THE LOWER SORT are slaves by nature: it is better for them, as for all inferiors, that they should live under the direction of a master. For he who can be—and therefore is—made someone else's property and he who is rational enough to accept authority but not to have it is a slave by nature… And indeed the use made of slaves and of tame animals is not very different… It is clear then that some men are by nature slaves and that to keep them as slaves is not just advantageous but right."

The Greek philosopher Aristotle (384–322 BCE) makes the case for slavery, suggesting that slaves are an inferior order of human and that they may actually need the direction of the more civilized Greeks.

14

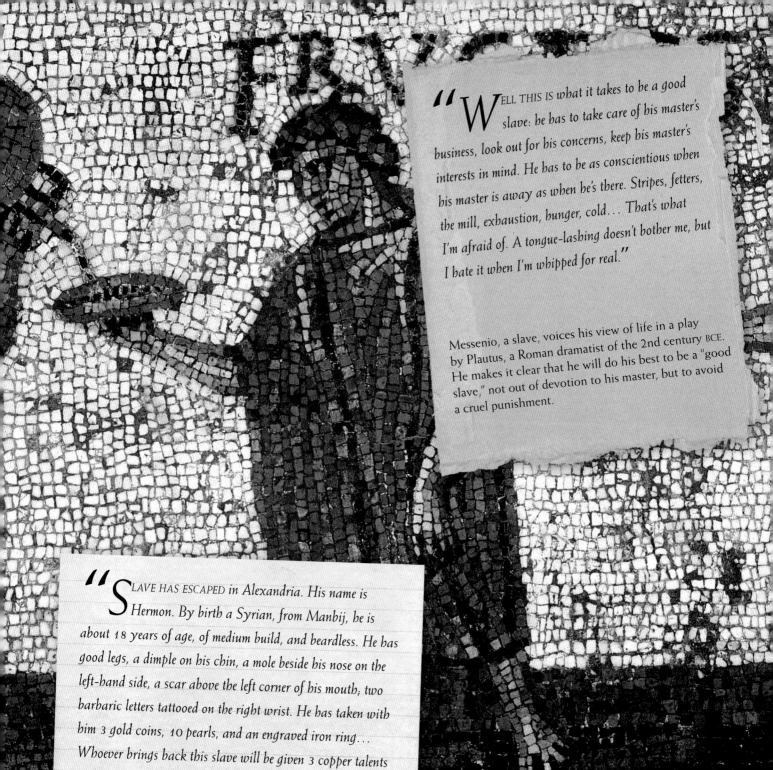

"WELL THIS IS what it takes to be a good slave: he has to take care of his master's business, look out for his concerns, keep his master's interests in mind. He has to be as conscientious when his master is away as when he's there. Stripes, fetters, the mill, exhaustion, hunger, cold… That's what I'm afraid of. A tongue-lashing doesn't bother me, but I hate it when I'm whipped for real."

Messenio, a slave, voices his view of life in a play by Plautus, a Roman dramatist of the 2nd century BCE. He makes it clear that he will do his best to be a "good slave," not out of devotion to his master, but to avoid a cruel punishment.

"SLAVE HAS ESCAPED in Alexandria. His name is Hermon. By birth a Syrian, from Manbij, he is about 18 years of age, of medium build, and beardless. He has good legs, a dimple on his chin, a mole beside his nose on the left-hand side, a scar above the left corner of his mouth, two barbaric letters tattooed on the right wrist. He has taken with him 3 gold coins, 10 pearls, and an engraved iron ring… Whoever brings back this slave will be given 3 copper talents as a reward; for pointing him out in a temple, 2 talents."

Aristogenes, son of Ambassador Chrysippus of Alabanda, offers a reward for the recapture of a runaway slave in this notice posted up in Alexandria, Egypt, around 100 BCE. Hermon has clearly taken some of his master's property, but his most serious theft is of his own self.

CHRISTIANS AND MUSLIMS

THE RISE OF CHRISTIANITY AND ISLAM changed attitudes to slavery, but certainly did not end it. Christianity, which first developed within the Roman Empire, accepted slavery as a fact of life. Islam, founded by the Prophet Muhammed in the 7th century, allowed its Muslim followers to enslave non-Muslims, but not to own other Muslims. Christians later agreed that they should not enslave fellow Christians, but made slaves of Muslims or of "heathens"—people of neither faith. During the Middle Ages, Muslims and Christians were almost always at war, each taking prisoners from the other side as slaves.

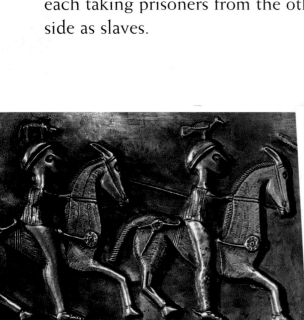

Slavs as slaves
Viking raiders captured Slavs in Russia and sold them as slaves to the Byzantine Empire, which became the most powerful state in the Christian world after the fall of the Roman Empire. Our word "slave" comes from "Slav."

Blond angels
A story about Gregory the Great (pope from 590 to 604 CE) concerns slaves in Christian Rome. When Gregory saw young Angles (people from Britain) for sale in a slave market, he said they were "Not Angles but angels."

Wealth from trading slaves
Venice was one of the many European cities that traded slaves, selling both to Muslims and Christians at great slave markets in the Mediterranean. Fortunes were made from this trade in people.

Slave soldiers

Muslim states used slaves to fight their wars. The Muslim Ottoman Empire forcibly took young boys from Christian Slav families of Europe and trained them as slave soldiers. Called Janissaries, they were the elite troops of the Ottoman army.

SERFS NOT SLAVES

In Christian countries of northern and western Europe, such as England and France, slavery largely died out during medieval times, although most people were still not "free" in the modern sense. The land was worked by peasants, called "serfs" (from the Latin word for slave). Serfs worked for their local lord and could not quit his service. But unlike slaves, serfs had certain rights. Most importantly, they could not be bought or sold separately from the land.

It is estimated that more than a million European Christians experienced slavery at the hands of North African Muslims between 1530 and 1780.

European slaves in Africa

North African ports such as Algiers and Tripoli had slave markets where Christian Europeans, captured by Muslim pirates or raiders, were sold. They were often freed when friends or relatives paid a ransom.

Battle of Lepanto

In 1571 a great battle was fought between Christian and Muslim galleys (warships with oars) at Lepanto in the Mediterranean. Both sides used galley slaves to row the boats. The victorious Christians freed 12,000 slaves held by the Muslims.

AFRICA AND SLAVERY

AT THE TIME of the European Middle Ages, great empires flourished in Africa, along with many small states and village societies. There was slavery in Africa just as in every other part of the world—prisoners of war, criminals, and people in debt were commonly forced into slavery. Thousands of enslaved Africans were sold to traders who carried them to Muslim countries on the Mediterranean coast and in the Middle East, where there was great demand for their labor.

African splendor
The wealth and sophistication of medieval African societies is shown by their art. For example, artisans in the kingdom of Benin, West Africa, created these fine bronze carvings of warriors for the ruler's palace.

Rich and powerful
The Muslim emperor of Mali was one of the most powerful African rulers. Mali's governers enslaved non-Muslim people living around their borders and used them to work the fields, or sold them to slave traders. Mansa Musa, emperor from 1312–1337, is seen here holding a nugget of gold.

Trading cities
Cities such as Timbuktu and Djenné in Mali stood at the western end of trade routes across the Sahara Desert. The mosque at Djenné stands on the site of an earlier mosque built in 1240, when the people of Mali converted to the Islamic faith. It reflects the wealth these cities earned by trading goods and slaves.

Slave caravans
Enslaved people bought in West African markets were transported across the Sahara desert by camel trains. The Tuareg nomads who lived in the desert played a major role in this cross-Saharan trade. Many slaves did not survive the long and grueling desert journey.

Slave trade routes in medieval Africa

▨ Sahara desert →→ Trade Routes

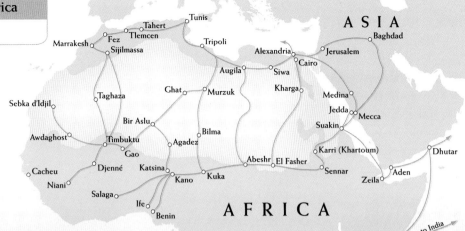

Medieval African slave routes

A network of trade routes linked West Africa with Morocco, Egypt, and the Middle East. Enslaved people from East Africa were transported by boat, chiefly to Arabia. These routes were used from around the 8th century for more than a thousand years.

THE CURSE OF HAM

Both Christians and Muslims encountered black Africans chiefly as slaves and came to view them as especially suited to slavery. They justified this attitude through a false interpretation of a story from the Bible. The story told how Noah put a curse upon the descendants of one of his sons, Ham. The interpretation, adopted by Christians and Muslims alike, claimed that Ham's descendants were people of dark skin, and that the curse made them inferior and so suitable for exploitation as slaves.

African slaves of Islam

In the Muslim countries of the Middle East, enslaved Africans performed the lowest types of manual work. This African slave is heaving a bucket of water from a well for his wealthy Arab owner.

"The Arabs have devastated our land, the land of Borno...
They have taken our free men and kin and they sell them
to the slave markets of Egypt, Syria, and elsewhere...
Our people are treated there as merchandise."

*King of Borno (northern Nigeria), in a letter to the sultan of Egypt,
pleading for the return of people stolen into slavery, written in 1391*

Muslim slave traders on horseback herd slave gangs in Africa

Royal backing
Voyages by Portuguese sailors were promoted by Portugal's royal rulers, especially Prince Henry the Navigator. From about 1420 Henry sent ships ever farther down the west coast of Africa, hoping to find the source of the gold and other valuable goods that he knew were traded across the Sahara.

EUROPEAN EXPLORATIONS

IN 1492, CHRISTOPHER COLUMBUS sailed with three ships across the Atlantic Ocean. This was a turning point in history, because it created a link between two parts of the world: the "Old World" of Europe, Asia, and Africa, and the "New World" of the Americas. Columbus's journey was one of many long-distance voyages made by countries such as Portugal, Spain, France, and England, whose rulers were eager to find lands to conquer, lucrative trade, and converts to Christianity. These voyages led to the growth of a large-scale slave trade across the Atlantic.

Voyages of exploration c.1450–1550

→ Spanish voyages
→ Portuguese voyages
→ English voyages
→ French voyages

Europe's major voyages of exploration c.1450–1550
In the 15th century Europeans developed the technology to make ocean voyages. The Portuguese were the first to sail around Africa to India. Other countries mounted voyages across the Atlantic. In 1522 the first ship sailed around the world.

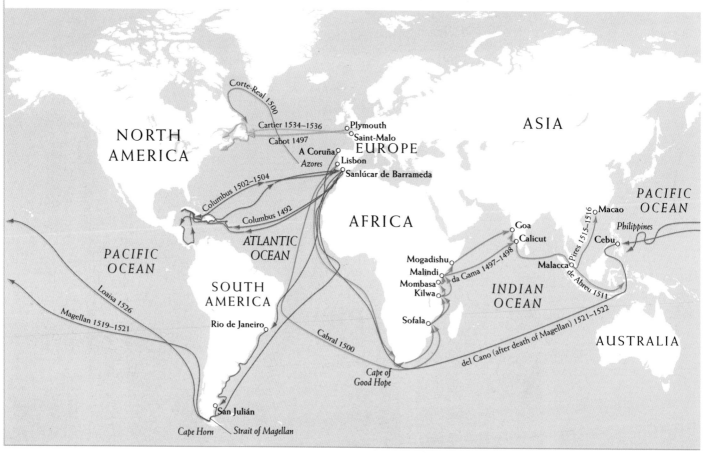

Ocean-going ships
Three-masted carracks and caravels were small—a caravel might be 65 ft (20 m) in length—but they could survive in heavy seas. Two of the ships with which Christopher Columbus crossed the Atlantic in 1492 were probably like this caravel.

Columbus arrives
Christopher Columbus was a sailor from Genoa in Italy. He won the backing of the rulers of Spain for a voyage westward to India. He did not know that the Americas lay between Europe and Asia in that direction. In 1492 he landed on an island in the Bahamas and claimed it for Spain.

Finding the way
To make oceanic voyages, European sailors needed to keep track of their position when out of sight of land. They usually navigated by observation of the Sun, planets, and stars, using primitive instruments such as the astrolabe to measure the height of these celestial bodies above the horizon. The magnetic compass (above), originally invented by the Chinese, was in use in Europe from the 13th century.

Strange encounter
To Columbus and the other sailors who followed in his wake, the plants, animals, and humans of the New World looked strange and exotic. Peoples such as the Caribs, who lived on Dominica and other West Indian islands, had customs and clothing unlike anything Europeans had ever encountered. The appearance and behavior of the Europeans was also a surprise to the native peoples.

CATASTROPHE IN THE AMERICAS

THE ARRIVAL OF EUROPEANS after Columbus's famous voyage of 1492 spelled disaster for the native peoples of the Americas. They had no immunity to the unfamiliar diseases that the strangers brought with them. Those who survived disease epidemics saw their societies destroyed by European invaders. Spanish adventurers, the conquistadores, overthrew the empires of the Aztecs in Mexico and the Incas in Peru. Native Americans were forced to work for their conquerors and were often victims of atrocities. Within a century, 80 percent of the indigenous population of the Americas had died.

In just one century, the Native American population fell from 50 million to just 10 million.

Inca gold
The motive for European conquests in the Americas was straightforward greed—the lust for precious metals. When the Spanish conquistador Francisco Pizarro seized control of the Inca Empire in Peru in 1532, he found many exquisite objects in silver and gold produced by Inca craftsmen.

America before Columbus
The native population of the Americas was varied, ranging from village societies in the Caribbean to wide-ranging empires on the American mainland. There were skilled craftsmen and farmers, fine temples, and prosperous towns. The Mexican city of Teotihuacán had a population of more than 100,000 at its peak, which was 1,000 years before the arrival of Columbus.

Guns and horses

The conquistadores had technological advantages that helped them defeat Native American warriors, despite being heavily outnumbered. These included steel weapons, armor, and primitive firearms, to set against the Native Americans' stone-tipped spears and arrows. The invaders also had horses, which were unknown in the Americas.

Ruthless ruler

Spanish conquistador Hernán Cortés overthrew the mighty Aztec Empire with just a handful of followers. He was able to do this partly through making alliances with other peoples in Mexico who hated the Aztecs. This image of Cortés fighting on horseback was made by an artist from one such allied people, the Tlaxcalans. They helped Cortés seize control of the Aztec capital Tenochtitlán in 1521.

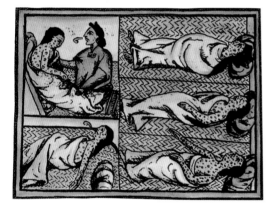

Laid waste by disease

The sufferings brought to the Native Americans by the arrival of Europeans are almost unimaginable. Disease caused devastation. Smallpox (above) and measles, unknown in the Americas, spread like wildfire, decimating populations that had no time to evolve natural defenses.

Opposing exploitation

Bartolomé de Las Casas was a Spanish priest who protested against the torture and murder of Native Americans. Largely through his influence, the Spanish monarchy attempted to prevent the enslavement and exploitation of native people in Spain's American colonies, passing the New Laws of 1542. Spanish colonists, in fact, continued to mistreat and overwork native people.

"My eyes have seen these acts so foreign to human nature, and now I tremble as I write… Who in future generations will believe this? I myself writing as a knowledgeable eyewitness can hardly believe it…"

Fray Bartolomé de Las Casas, 1542

Enslaved Indians are beaten as they carry supplies during Spanish expeditions in America, 1591

SETTLEMENT AND EXPLOITATION

IN THE 1500S AND 1600S, European colonies took shape in the Americas. The continent offered a potential source of great wealth, with plentiful natural resources. But these riches could not be exploited without people to work in the fields and mines and perform other tasks. Only limited numbers of European settlers were prepared to cross the Atlantic, and the high death rate of Native Americans reduced their value as slave laborers. In 1510, King Ferdinand of Spain authorized the import of enslaved Africans into the Americas. The labor to build the American colonies would come from Africa.

Dividing the Americas
In the Treaty of Tordesillas in 1494, Pope Alexander VI divided newly discovered lands between Portugal and Spain. In the Americas this division gave Brazil to Portugal and handed the rest to Spain. But the English, French, and Dutch ignored the pope's decision and contested the Portuguese and Spanish claims to control the Americas.

European possessions
By 1650, European states claimed control of large areas of the Americas. Spain and Portugal held South and Central America. Eastern North America was mostly colonized by the English and French—although New Amsterdam was a Dutch possession. The Caribbean was fought over by competing European powers.

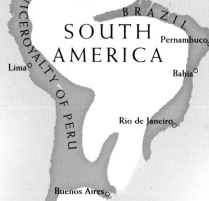

NORTH AMERICA

HUDSON'S BAY COMPANY

NEW FRANCE

Québec

ENGLISH COLONIES

New Amsterdam

ATLANTIC OCEAN

VICEROYALTY OF NEW SPAIN

Mexico City

PACIFIC OCEAN

SOUTH AMERICA

BRAZIL

Pernambuco

Lima

Bahia

VICEROYALTY OF PERU

Rio de Janeiro

Buenos Aires

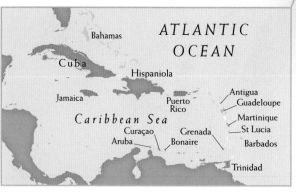

Bahamas

ATLANTIC OCEAN

Cuba

Hispaniola

Jamaica

Puerto Rico

Antigua
Guadeloupe

Martinique

St Lucia

Caribbean Sea

Curaçao

Grenada

Aruba

Bonaire

Barbados

Trinidad

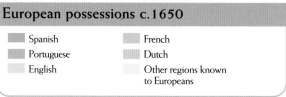

European possessions c.1650

Spanish	French
Portuguese	Dutch
English	Other regions known to Europeans

Capital city

Mexico City was the capital of the Viceroyalty of New Spain, which administered the northern part of Spain's possessions in the Americas. Its population of government officials and other wealthy Spaniards required servants and artisans to provide for their needs. Few Native Americans were brought into the city. Instead, the Spanish imported enslaved Africans to fulfill these roles. By the 17th century, enslaved Africans made up almost half the population of Mexico City, working as gardeners, cooks, coachmen, carpenters, masons, and weavers.

English colonists in North America

The colonies established by England in North America were either founded by enterprising wealthy people in search of profit or by independent-minded religious groups. The Pilgrims and the Puritans who settled in New England in the 1620s and 1630s were chiefly interested in the freedom to practice their Protestant faiths as they saw fit. These New Englanders did import enslaved Africans, but in far smaller numbers than the colonies farther south.

Brazilian slavery

In Portuguese-ruled Brazil, as in the Spanish colonies, only small numbers of Europeans settled. At first Native Americans provided a supply of workers—mostly as slaves—but when the exploitation of Brazil's natural resources and farming potential expanded in the late 1500s, the import of slaves from Africa developed on a large scale. Here, enslaved Africans are being used to mine diamonds, watched by supervisors with whips.

INDENTURED SERVANTS

Colonists in North America brought in "indentured servants" to do their hard work. These were poor Europeans who signed a contract binding them to work for a master for three to seven years in return for payment of their passage across the Atlantic. Like slaves, they were often treated with cruelty. Some indentured servants found it difficult to leave their master's service even when the term was up.

THE ATLANTIC SLAVE TRADE

THE SETTLEMENT AND EXPLOITATION of the New World by Europeans led to more and more enslaved Africans being shipped across the ocean from Africa to the Americas until there were more slaves than ever before in human history. For hundreds of years, the traffic in slaves was accepted by almost everyone as normal. The sufferings of the enslaved were ignored.

Sailing into New York Harbor
Enslaved Africans, brought by ship to New Amsterdam (later New York) as early as 1626, helped build the city. In 1664, when the British took New Amsterdam from the Dutch, 500 African slaves lived in the city.

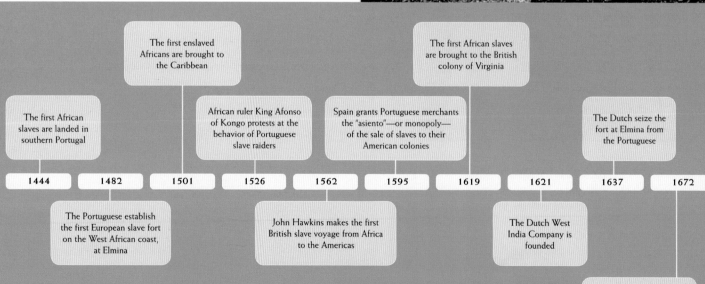

The first enslaved Africans are brought to the Caribbean

The first African slaves are brought to the British colony of Virginia

The first African slaves are landed in southern Portugal

African ruler King Afonso of Kongo protests at the behavior of Portuguese slave raiders

Spain grants Portuguese merchants the "asiento"—or monopoly— of the sale of slaves to their American colonies

The Dutch seize the fort at Elmina from the Portuguese

| 1444 | 1482 | 1501 | 1526 | 1562 | 1595 | 1619 | 1621 | 1637 | 1672 |

The Portuguese establish the first European slave fort on the West African coast, at Elmina

John Hawkins makes the first British slave voyage from Africa to the Americas

The Dutch West India Company is founded

The Royal African Company (RAC) is given a monopoly of British slave trading

30

Ships from the North American colony of Rhode Island join in the Atlantic slave trade

The RAC monopoly ends and slave trading is thrown open to all British merchants

The Atlantic slave trade reaches its peak, with 80,000 enslaved Africans embarked every year

Britain and the United States make the slave trade illegal

Brazil is the last country officially to ban the Atlantic slave trade

| 1698 | c.1700 | 1709 | c.1740 | 1775–1800 | 1787 | 1807–08 | 1825–50 | 1851 | 1866 |

The Asante kingdom emerges as a slave-trading power on the West African coast

A mass campaign for the abolition of the slave trade is launched in Britain

Almost 70,000 slaves a year are shipped from Africa, despite the slave-trade ban

The Atlantic slave trade effectively ends

Liverpool overtakes Bristol as Britain's—and the world's—main slave-trading port

PORTUGUESE PRELUDE

PORTUGUESE VOYAGERS WHO SAILED DOWN the west coast of Africa in the 1400s brought back enslaved Africans for sale. The first human cargo was landed at Lagos in southern Portugal in 1444. By 1540 some 12,000 slaves a year were being imported into Europe in Portuguese ships. Enslaved Africans made up one in ten of the population of Portugal's capital, Lisbon. The importing of slaves into Europe subsequently declined, but the slave trade grew, as the Portuguese began to carry enslaved Africans across the Atlantic to the Americas.

African fort
The Portuguese established the first European fort on the African coast at Elmina in modern-day Ghana in 1482. The fort was not used to defend the Portuguese against Africans, but against rival European powers. The Portuguese could only trade in Africa with the permission of local rulers since they were outnumbered and had no military advantage over African states.

Royal ally
Portugal established good relations with some West African rulers. Nzinga Mvemba, known to the Portuguese as Afonso I, was the ruler of the kingdom of Kongo from 1509. He exchanged ambassadors with the king of Portugal and agreed to be baptized a Catholic. The Portuguese gave the Kongolese king this European-style coat of arms.

Powerful protest
Kongolese King Nzinga Mvemba allowed Portuguese traders to live in his country, although they had to show respect to such a powerful ruler. Since slavery existed in Kongo, the king accepted the sale of African slaves to the Portuguese. But in 1526 he protested against the behavior of Portuguese traders, accusing them of kidnapping free Africans for sale as slaves and depopulating his kingdom.

Buying slaves in Africa

Although the Portuguese sometimes kidnapped free Africans, or organized armed raids on villages, they also purchased slaves from other traders whenever they could. They used goods brought with them from Portugal to barter—or exchange—for the slaves, or paid for them with West African money such as metal bracelets called "manillas."

WEALTHY CITY

Portugal's rulers grew rich on the wealth of trade, especially the trade in slaves. The king received a percentage of the price of every slave sold. Many fine buildings were constructed in the capital, Lisbon, paid for partly with the profits from the slave trade. They included the Jerónimos Monastery, built in the 1500s, and now a UNESCO World Heritage Site.

Tokens of trade

Manillas were worn by African women to display their husbands' wealth. The Portuguese made copies in Europe to ship to Africa, where they became the main token of exchange for slaves.

Sugar plantations

The Portuguese used enslaved Africans to grow sugar cane and other crops on plantations—large estates—on Atlantic islands such as Madeira. Slave-produced sugar proved highly profitable and the Madeira plantation model was imitated on a vastly larger scale in the Americas.

RISE OF THE ATLANTIC SLAVE TRADE

THROUGH THE 1500S AND 1600S the trade in enslaved Africans across the Atlantic swelled from a trickle to a flood, as European colonists in the Americas found demand for plantation labor soaring. Portugal was the first leader in the trade, carrying thousands of slaves to Brazil and the Spanish Empire in the Americas. But other Europeans—British, French, Dutch, and Danes—soon muscled in, establishing bases on the West African coast and fighting for control of American colonies. By 1700, the slave trade was an established part of economic life on both sides of the Atlantic.

John Hawkins
The first Englishman to play a significant part in the Atlantic slave trade was John Hawkins. The Spanish wanted to shut the English out of trade with their American colonies, but in 1562 Hawkins obtained a cargo of Africans by theft, raids, and trade on the West African coast. He succeeded in selling it in the Americas.

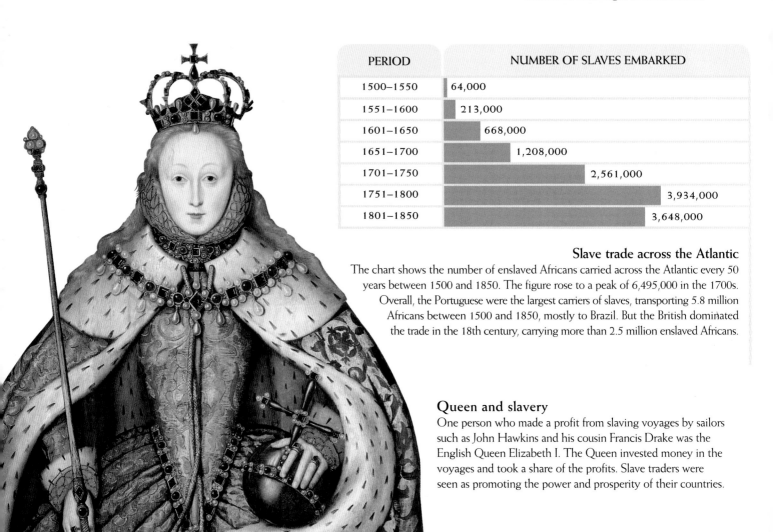

PERIOD	NUMBER OF SLAVES EMBARKED
1500–1550	64,000
1551–1600	213,000
1601–1650	668,000
1651–1700	1,208,000
1701–1750	2,561,000
1751–1800	3,934,000
1801–1850	3,648,000

Slave trade across the Atlantic
The chart shows the number of enslaved Africans carried across the Atlantic every 50 years between 1500 and 1850. The figure rose to a peak of 6,495,000 in the 1700s. Overall, the Portuguese were the largest carriers of slaves, transporting 5.8 million Africans between 1500 and 1850, mostly to Brazil. But the British dominated the trade in the 18th century, carrying more than 2.5 million enslaved Africans.

Queen and slavery
One person who made a profit from slaving voyages by sailors such as John Hawkins and his cousin Francis Drake was the English Queen Elizabeth I. The Queen invested money in the voyages and took a share of the profits. Slave traders were seen as promoting the power and prosperity of their countries.

Dutch West India Company

In the early 17th century, the Dutch were the world's finest sailors—and aggressive enemies of the Spanish and Portuguese. The Dutch West India Company was set up by Dutch merchants to trade in the Caribbean and the rest of the Americas. Enslaved Africans were one of their main cargoes. Their profits allowed them to construct this fine headquarters in Amsterdam.

From 1500 to 1800, four-fifths of all people who crossed the Atlantic to the Americas were enslaved Africans.

Slave-trading fort

Forts built on the African coast often changed hands as European countries fought each other for control of trade. Cape Coast Castle in Ghana was originally founded by the Swedish Africa Company, but was taken over by Denmark, then captured by the British in 1664.

Royal African Company

In 1672 the British monarchy and London merchants founded the Royal African Company. Its charter granted it a monopoly—complete control—of trade in African slaves. The company transported some 5,000 enslaved Africans across the Atlantic every year, mostly to Britain's West Indian colonies, before losing its monopoly in 1698.

Building New Amsterdam

The Dutch were the first Europeans to bring enslaved Africans to North America on a substantial scale. The foundations of the Dutch settlement of New Amsterdam—later renamed New York—were laid by African laborers brought in on ships by the Dutch West India Company.

THE SLAVE TRADE AT ITS PEAK

THE ATLANTIC SLAVE TRADE reached its peak in the 18th century. By the 1780s, 80,000 to 100,000 enslaved Africans were being forcibly transported to the Americas every year. They provided the massive labor force required to produce sugar, coffee, tobacco, and cocoa on plantations in the Americas. Growing demand for these small luxuries in the cities of Europe and North America made them profitable items of trade. So slavery expanded to satisfy European consumers and enrich merchants and bankers.

Bitter sweet
Sugar plantations created the first large-scale demand for enslaved Africans in the Americas. Sugar production spread from Brazil to the Caribbean islands, where British-owned Barbados and Jamaica and French-owned Martinique and Guadeloupe became major sugar producers. As work on sugar plantations was so hard, slaves died in large numbers. They were replaced by newly purchased slaves.

Coffee houses
In 18th-century Europe, coffee houses were the place for men to meet, read newspapers, and discuss the events of the day. They were central to the lifestyle of the city-dwelling elite. But the coffee these people drank was produced by slave labor. Customers rarely thought about the origin of the products they enjoyed.

CONSUMER PRODUCE	
	Sugar European consumption of sugar rose dramatically—in Britain from 2 lb (0.9 kg) per person in 1650 to 24 lb (10.9 kg) per person by 1800.
	Coffee In 1750 Britain imported 270 lb (123 kg) of coffee from the West Indies; by 1775 the figure was almost 60,000 lb (27,215 kg).
	Cocoa This was used by the Spanish to make drinking chocolate from the 16th century—a habit that spread to France and Britain. Chocolate for eating appeared in the 18th century.
	Tobacco British imports of Virginian tobacco grew from 60,000 lb (27,215 kg) in 1620 to 76 million lb (34.5 million kg) a year in the late 18th century.

Rise of consumerism

Between 1650 and 1800, the British became among the main consumers of slave-produced goods. Sugar was the most important plantation product, but consumption of coffee and cocoa (as a warm drink and to make chocolate) was increasing. Tobacco imports saw a consistently high growth year-on-year, with the port of Chesapeake, Virginia, exporting 38 million pounds (17,273 million kg) by 1700.

New England traders

North Americans—from Rhode Island and Massachusetts especially—became heavily involved in the slave trade. By 1750 over 20 ships were sailing from the small colony of Rhode Island to Africa each year. They not only went to Africa to buy enslaved Africans and carry them back across the Atlantic, but also supplied goods to the British slave plantations of the Caribbean—including corn, salted fish, rum, and lumber.

Britain dominant

Almost half of the slaves brought across the Atlantic in the 18th century were carried by the British, a reflection of the growing strength of Britain's shipping and finance. The ship painted on this earthenware bowl was based at the port of Liverpool in northern England.

Slavery in North America

Only a small percentage of the slaves carried across the Atlantic went to Britain's North American colonies. Still, ports such as Charleston in South Carolina were major importers of enslaved Africans. This slave auction is taking place in Virginia, where tobacco was the main crop.

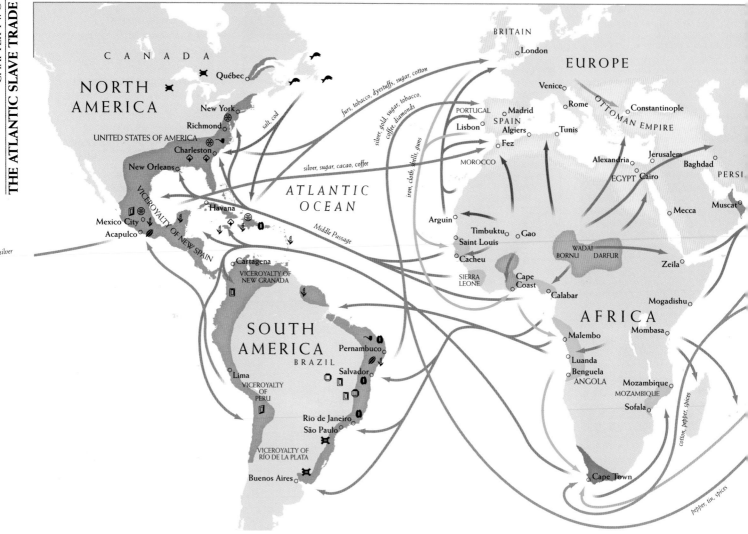

Map labels:
CANADA
NORTH AMERICA
Québec
New York
Richmond
UNITED STATES OF AMERICA
Charleston
New Orleans
Mexico City
Acapulco
Havana
VICEROYALTY OF NEW SPAIN
Cartagena
VICEROYALTY OF NEW GRANADA
SOUTH AMERICA
BRAZIL
Pernambuco
Lima
VICEROYALTY OF PERU
Salvador
Rio de Janeiro
São Paulo
VICEROYALTY OF RÍO DE LA PLATA
Buenos Aires

ATLANTIC OCEAN
Middle Passage

BRITAIN
London
EUROPE
Venice
Rome
Constantinople
PORTUGAL
Madrid
Lisbon
SPAIN
Algiers
OTTOMAN EMPIRE
Tunis
MOROCCO
Fez
Alexandria
Jerusalem
Baghdad
PERSIA
EGYPT
Cairo
Mecca
Muscat
Arguin
Timbuktu
Gao
Saint Louis
Cacheu
WADAI
BORNU
DARFUR
Zeila
SIERRA LEONE
Cape Coast
Calabar
Mogadishu
AFRICA
Malembo
Mombasa
Luanda
Benguela
ANGOLA
Mozambique
MOZAMBIQUE
Sofala
Cape Town

furs, tobacco, dyestuffs, sugar, cotton
silver, gold, sugar, tobacco, coffee, diamonds
silver, sugar, cacao, coffee
iron, cloth, shells, guns
salt, cod
silver
cotton, pepper, spices
pepper, tin, spices

PATTERNS OF TRADE

THE ATLANTIC SLAVE TRADE involved more than simply carrying human cargo. European and North American traders bought goods to exchange for enslaved Africans, ranging from European items to cotton cloth from India. The products of the slave-worked plantations in the Americas were sold mostly in Europe. Merchants engaged in slaving maximized profits through "triangular trades": a ship might set off from Britain carrying trade goods, which were exchanged in Africa for slaves, who were then sold in the Caribbean. The ship might return home with a cargo of sugar.

Made for Africa
European manufacturers often produced goods specifically to be traded with Africans in return for slaves. Firearms made in Britain are a prime example. They were part of a policy of promoting armed conflict in Africa, which, in turn, increased the flow of captives to European ships.

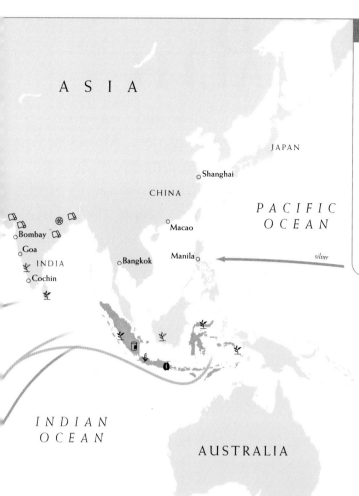

A S I A

JAPAN

Shanghai

CHINA

PACIFIC
OCEAN

Macao

Bombay

Goa

Bangkok

Manila

silver

INDIA

Cochin

INDIAN
OCEAN

AUSTRALIA

The World Slave Trade 1400–1860

- major slave-trading nation
- export center for African slaves
- export center for Muslim slaves
- distribution of African slaves
- distribution of Muslim slaves
- African nations with active slave trade

- → routes of European slave traders
- → routes of Ottoman slave traders
- → routes of Saharan slave traders
- → routes of Arab slave traders
- → exports of Muslim slaves from Southeast Asia
- → goods exported in exchange for slaves
- → goods exported for slaves
- → European exports to Africa

Goods produced using slaves
- cacao
- coffee
- cotton
- diamonds
- gold
- silver
- sugar
- tobacco

Other goods traded
- dyestuffs
- furs and hides
- pepper
- silk and textiles
- spices
- tin

Goods imported for slaves
- salted cod

Rum and slaves
New England traders developed their own "triangular trade," buying molasses—a by-product of sugar manufacture—in the Caribbean, using it to make rum in New England, then taking the rum to Africa to exchange for slaves. The slaves were then sold in the Caribbean, after which the traders shipped another cargo of molasses.

Complex exchanges
By the 18th century, European and North American ships linked far-flung areas of the world in a web of trade routes. The trade in slaves across the Atlantic and the products of slave labor in the Americas were at the heart of this system.

In the late 18th century, Britain was exporting about 300,000 muskets a year to Africa.

Busy Bristol
Merchants in the port of Bristol in the west of England equipped ships for slave-trading voyages to West Africa, and imported large quantities of goods produced on slave-worked plantations in Britain's colonies in the West Indies and North America. Bristol grew to be the second-largest city in Britain by 1800.

Prosperous ports

Port cities such as Liverpool and Bristol in England, Lisbon in Portugal, Newport in Rhode Island, and Charleston in South Carolina grew rich on the trade in slaves and slave produce. Some of this wealth was invested in fine buildings such as this theater in Nantes, a city that controlled most of the French slave trade.

A WORLD OF WEALTH

IN THE 18TH CENTURY, the Atlantic slave trade was not considered a shameful or illegitimate business. Money was put into slaving voyages by upstanding citizens of Boston, Massachusetts, by members of the British royal family, and by ordinary artisans or shopkeepers with savings to invest. Men from respectable families might run a sugar plantation or captain a slave ship. Money and goods from the slave system were everywhere in the booming economies of Europe and the Americas.

Financing slavery

Wealthy financiers who put up large sums of money to promote slave voyages could make substantial profits without seeing anything of the suffering and brutality of the trade, which happened far away. Sir Francis Baring—portrayed here on the left with his two business partners—was one of many bankers in the City of London who made fortunes out of investment in slavery.

Making a living

For every individual in Europe or North America who grew rich on slavery, there were thousands who depended upon the slave trade for their living in a more modest way. The sailmakers, ropemakers, carpenters, shopkeepers, and sailors of a busy Atlantic port such as Liverpool almost all lived to some degree off the proceeds of the trade.

Anglican slaver

John Newton became famous as a preacher in the Anglican church and is remembered today as the author of the hymn "Amazing Grace." But as a young man in the 1750s he had been a slave-ship captain. At the time he had no misgivings about it, although later in his life he denounced the trade.

Philosopher of liberty

John Locke was a thinker whose ideas on freedom were to inspire the revolt of American colonists against British rule that led to the founding of the United States. But Locke was a shareholder in the slave trading Royal African Company.

Respectable slavery

Some merchants and landowners became extremely wealthy on slave trade proceeds. Harewood House in Yorkshire, northern England, is one of Britain's most famous stately homes. The Lascelles family, who built it in the 18th century, were involved in sugar and slave trading, and became major plantation owners in Barbados and Jamaica. At their peak they owned almost 3,000 slaves.

William Beckford (1760–1844), a British aristocrat, earned the equivalent of about six million dollars a year from his family plantations in the West Indies.

"I think I should have quitted it [the slave trade] sooner, had I considered it, as I now do, to be unlawful and wrong. But I never had a scruple on this head at the time; nor was such a thought once suggested to me by a friend."

John Newton writes as a former slave trader-turned-abolitionist, in his pamphlet Thoughts Upon the African Slave Trade, *1788*

THE IMPACT ON AFRICA

MOST OF THE ENSLAVED AFRICANS carried across the Atlantic were bought from the rulers and merchants of the West African coast. Some African states refused to trade slaves, but others saw it as an opportunity. Coastal kingdoms such as Dahomey, Oyo, and Asante grew rich on the spoils of the slave trade, which became their principal activity. Using guns supplied by the Europeans, they waged wars or sent out raiding parties to capture people for sale. These constant raids depopulated large areas of Africa far inland.

Friendly relations

European and North American traders had to establish friendly relations with African rulers and merchants. They brought them gifts and in return were invited to feasts. They even on occasion took the sons of African merchants back to Europe or North America to live in their houses. Both sides saw themselves as engaged in business and were indifferent to the fate of the humans they bought and sold.

Sharp traders

Africans were demanding traders who only supplied slaves if they were offered high-quality goods in exchange. In addition to practical items such as salt, iron pots, knives, and firearms, they liked Asian silks, American rum (left), and French brandy. They accepted cowrie shells, brought from the Indian Ocean, as money. In about 1760, approximately 80,000 cowries would buy a slave.

Imported food

The opening up of trade routes between Africa and the Americas affected what Africans ate. Cassava (above) and maize were important crops brought to Africa from the New World. They soon became staple African foods, and remain so to this day.

Kingdom of gold

The Asante kingdom became wealthy through trade in slaves, obtained mostly as prisoners through aggressive warfare. The Asante did not see themselves as enslaving fellow "Africans"—they regarded black people of other ethnic groups as foreigners. The Asante king sat on a gold throne and Asante artisans made figures of solid gold.

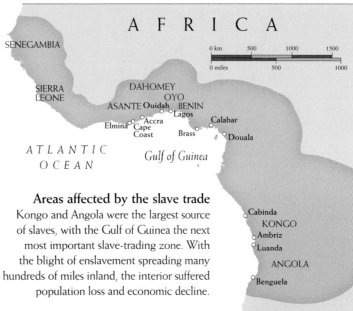

Areas affected by the slave trade

Kongo and Angola were the largest source of slaves, with the Gulf of Guinea the next most important slave-trading zone. With the blight of enslavement spreading many hundreds of miles inland, the interior suffered population loss and economic decline.

West African slave trade

■ Region of slave trade activity in West Africa

Merchants of Bonny River

The Africans who traded with Europeans were not always part of warlike states. The British obtained many slaves from the African merchant families of Bonny and Calabar, who were traders rather than warriors. They bought their slaves from inland and sold them on to the Europeans. Slave ships anchored in the Bonny River while a human cargo was assembled.

Easy targets

The Africans who were victims of the slave trade often lived far from the coast. They were easy prey since they did not have European-supplied guns and generally lived in small villages. The search for slaves inevitably ranged wider and wider as some areas became depopulated and the demand for slaves increased.

VOICES ON THE AFRICAN COAST

Buying slaves on the West African coast was a business both for those who bought and those who sold. Africans soon became fluent in foreign languages and exchanged polite letters with merchants in Europe and North America. Yet it was a business in which suffering and death were ever-present, not only for the victims, but also for traders and seamen exposed to disease during long stays on the tropical coast.

"As you are appointed commander of our new ship the Essex on board such we have shipped a well assorted cargo for the Windward Coast of Africa... barter your cargo for prime young slaves, none less than 4 ft 4 in [1.32 m] high... stay on Windward coast if trade brisk and can get away in 4 to 5 months... A few presents to the [African] traders now and then will not be lost, and will promote your trade and quick dispatch... for lying long on the coast brings distemper [illness] into your ship and often proves very fatal in the end..."

In 1784, Captain Peter Potter took the slave ship the Essex to West Africa on behalf of Liverpool merchant William Davenport. These were the instructions that Davenport wrote to Potter before he set out.

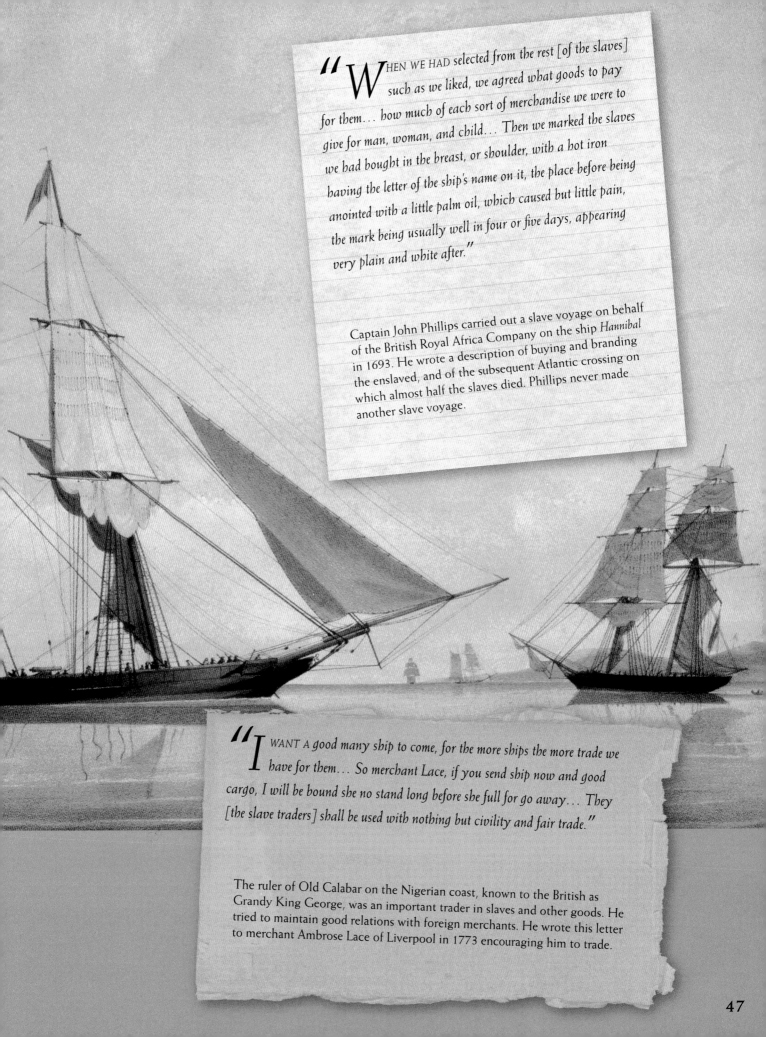

"WHEN WE HAD selected from the rest [of the slaves] such as we liked, we agreed what goods to pay for them... how much of each sort of merchandise we were to give for man, woman, and child... Then we marked the slaves we had bought in the breast, or shoulder, with a hot iron having the letter of the ship's name on it, the place before being anointed with a little palm oil, which caused but little pain, the mark being usually well in four or five days, appearing very plain and white after."

Captain John Phillips carried out a slave voyage on behalf of the British Royal Africa Company on the ship *Hannibal* in 1693. He wrote a description of buying and branding the enslaved, and of the subsequent Atlantic crossing on which almost half the slaves died. Phillips never made another slave voyage.

"I WANT A good many ship to come, for the more ships the more trade we have for them... So merchant Lace, if you send ship now and good cargo, I will be bound she no stand long before she full for go away... They [the slave traders] shall be used with nothing but civility and fair trade."

The ruler of Old Calabar on the Nigerian coast, known to the British as Grandy King George, was an important trader in slaves and other goods. He tried to maintain good relations with foreign merchants. He wrote this letter to merchant Ambrose Lace of Liverpool in 1773 encouraging him to trade.

COUNTING THE COST

THE SCALE OF THE TRANSATLANTIC slave trade is almost inconceivable. Although outlawed by many countries in the early 19th century, a large-scale Atlantic slave trade continued into the 1860s. By that time it is estimated that 12.5 million Africans had embarked on slave ships, of whom 10.7 million survived the Atlantic crossing. Since many captives died in Africa on marches to the coast, or awaiting shipment, the number actually enslaved may have been between 15 and 20 million. The survivors created a new population of African origin throughout the Americas.

SLAVE IMPORTS	
Brazil	4,864,000
British Caribbean	2,318,000
Spanish America	1,293,000
French Caribbean	1,120,000
Mainland North America	389,000

Where enslaved people went
Almost half of the 10.7 million enslaved Africans who arrived in the Americas were taken to Brazil. British and French islands in the West Indies were another major destination. A large proportion of the slaves carried to Spanish America went to Cuba. The United States took less than four percent of slaves imported to the Americas.

At the trade's peak 10,000 enslaved Africans were dying on Atlantic crossings each year.

African population
The long-term impact of the slave trade on population levels in Africa is disputed, since there are no accurate figures available for those times. However, those regions most subjected to slave-raiding must have been significantly depopulated by the trade. Best estimates suggest that in West Africa as a whole, the population did not actually fall, but natural population growth was slowed or halted.

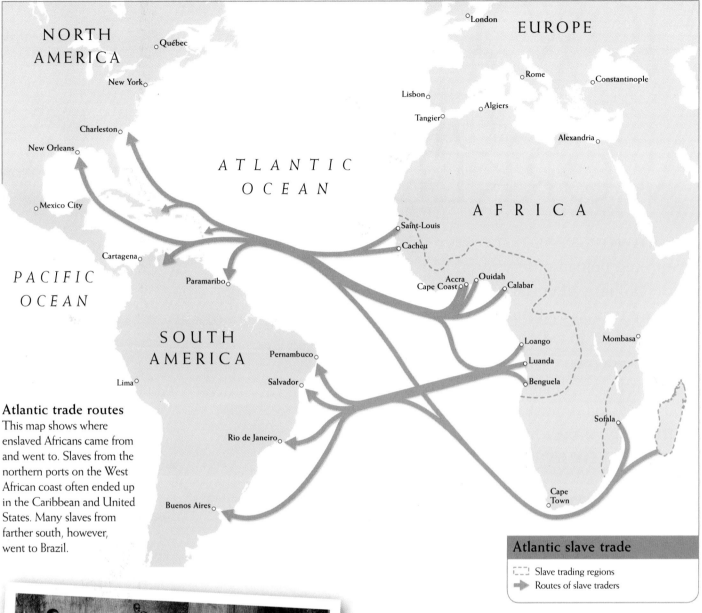

Atlantic trade routes

This map shows where enslaved Africans came from and went to. Slaves from the northern ports on the West African coast often ended up in the Caribbean and United States. Many slaves from farther south, however, went to Brazil.

Atlantic slave trade

- ⌐ ¬ Slave trading regions
- ➡ Routes of slave traders

Death toll

The precise cost of the slave trade in African lives cannot be established. An estimated 1.8 million enslaved Africans died on Atlantic voyages over four centuries, an average death toll of about 14 percent of those who embarked. But very large numbers died in Africa before embarkation, and countless more died within a few months of arrival in the Americas.

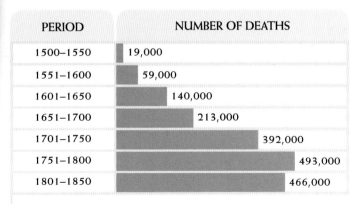

PERIOD	NUMBER OF DEATHS
1500–1550	19,000
1551–1600	59,000
1601–1650	140,000
1651–1700	213,000
1701–1750	392,000
1751–1800	493,000
1801–1850	466,000

African deaths at sea

In the early years of the Atlantic trade, only small numbers of enslaved Africans were embarked. But death rates were high—about one in five up to the 1650s. By the late 18th century, the death rate had fallen to under one in ten, but the number of people carried by ship was far higher.

HOW THE SLAVE TRADE WORKED

THE ATLANTIC SLAVE TRADE was a system for turning human misery into financial profit. Millions of enslaved Africans were violently torn away from their familiar lives and their loved ones. As "goods," they were deprived of their freedom and their basic humanity. Hundreds of thousands died of mistreatment and disease on the long journey from their villages across the ocean to the Americas.

The start of a terrible journey into slavery
At West African ports, Africans were forced by traders on to slave ships. Here, white men brutally separate an African family. Strong men often fetched a better price than women and children.

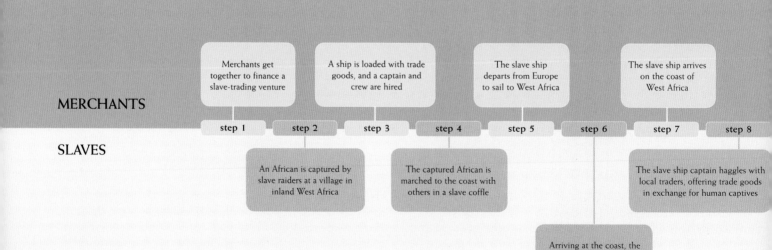

MERCHANTS

| step 1 | step 2 | step 3 | step 4 | step 5 | step 6 | step 7 | step 8 |

Merchants get together to finance a slave-trading venture

A ship is loaded with trade goods, and a captain and crew are hired

The slave ship departs from Europe to sail to West Africa

The slave ship arrives on the coast of West Africa

SLAVES

An African is captured by slave raiders at a village in inland West Africa

The captured African is marched to the coast with others in a slave coffle

The slave ship captain haggles with local traders, offering trade goods in exchange for human captives

Arriving at the coast, the African captives are held in a barracoon, ready for sale

With its human cargo confined below decks, the slave ship sets sail from the coast

Captives are purchased by slave ship captains; some are branded

The slave ship arrives off a West Indian island or the coast of the American mainland

The human cargo is sold on the deck of the ship or by auction on land

Slave owners take their newly purchased captives to plantations and put them to work

step 9   step 10   step 11   step 12   step 13   step 14   step 15   step 16   step 17

The Middle Passage: the ship carries its captives across the Atlantic ocean, a voyage of some six weeks

The ship takes on a cargo of export goods and sets off back to Europe

The African captives are held by the European slave traders on board ship or on land while enough slaves are purchased to make a full cargo

Surviving captives are prepared for sale; sometimes their bodies are oiled to make them appear healthier

51

Village people
Most Africans lived in villages. Every enslaved African had once had a clear identity within such a society—a hunter or a farmer, someone's husband or wife, son or daughter. From this familiar life they were brutally torn away to become simply a piece of saleable property.

BECOMING ENSLAVED

SLAVERY EXISTED WITHIN AFRICA at the time of the Atlantic slave trade. But on the whole Africans on the coast did not sell their personal slaves—these were people who had become enslaved as a result of debt or poverty and were regarded as part of a big extended family. To feed the demand for slaves to be carried across the Atlantic, they depended instead on warfare or raiding inland. A typical victim destined for the Atlantic slave trade was made captive in some violent way. He or she was then marched to the coast and held there, awaiting sale to the traders from overseas.

Men of war
Africa was not a peaceful continent. African warriors prided themselves on their fighting skills and warfare was common between neighboring peoples. When prisoners were taken they were either killed or made household slaves. The coming of the Europeans gave those prisoners an extra value to the warring tribes. It even led to more fighting, with the specific aim of taking prisoners for sale.

Raiding parties
Individuals were kidnapped as they went about their daily lives. Raiding parties would hide outside a village and wait for a chance to ambush victims. The raiders took their captives away from their old homes as quickly as possible. African rulers tried, without success, to limit this terrible human theft.

HOUSE OF SLAVES

The House of Slaves on Gorée Island off the coast of Senegal, West Africa, has become a much-visited memorial to the victims of the slave trade. Several thousand enslaved Africans were shipped from Gorée through the 18th century. The House of Slaves, built in 1776, was the home of a wealthy trader. Inside the house is the famous "Door of No Return" through which enslaved people were said to leave. There is no evidence of this, however.

The barracoons

When enslaved people from the interior arrived at a coastal slave-trading station, they were often held in large enclosures, known as barracoons, to await the arrival of European slave ships. Men were kept chained; women and children were held separately.

Bonds of slavery

Chains used to restrain captives were made from wrought iron and included leg irons, handcuffs, and, shown here, neck collars. Most were made in Britain.

Long chains were used to shackle up to 50 enslaved captives at a time.

Death march

Once taken prisoner, an enslaved person faced a terrible march often of hundreds of miles to the coast. The prisoners were shackled together in a line known as a coffle. They might be sold several times during this journey, making a profit for each new "owner" with every sale.

BUYERS AND SELLERS

SLAVE TRADING WAS A COMPLEX business operation. Merchants in Europe or North America worked to equip a ship for a voyage that might last a year or more. They bought trade goods and hired a captain to be responsible for sailing the ship and the buying and selling of slaves. When the ship reached the African coast, trading was complicated. The supply of enslaved Africans was not guaranteed, and experienced African merchants struck a hard bargain with the foreign buyers. The humanity of the Africans being bought and sold was ignored by all concerned.

Captains after fortune
The captain of a slave ship carried a heavy responsibility for the success of the enterprise. Most captains were on commission—if the voyage ended in a substantial profit, the captain could expect a handsome payoff, either in cash or in slaves given to him to sell on his own account.

Unhappy sailors
It was hard to recruit crew for slave ships. Conditions were poor—the death rate among sailors on slave voyages was as bad as that among the enslaved Africans. Often seamen were tricked into service—lured into debt and then forced to serve on slave ships to pay what they owed. Many deserted when they got a chance, in Africa or the Americas.

On average one in eight sailors on a slave ship died on a voyage, mainly from tropical diseases.

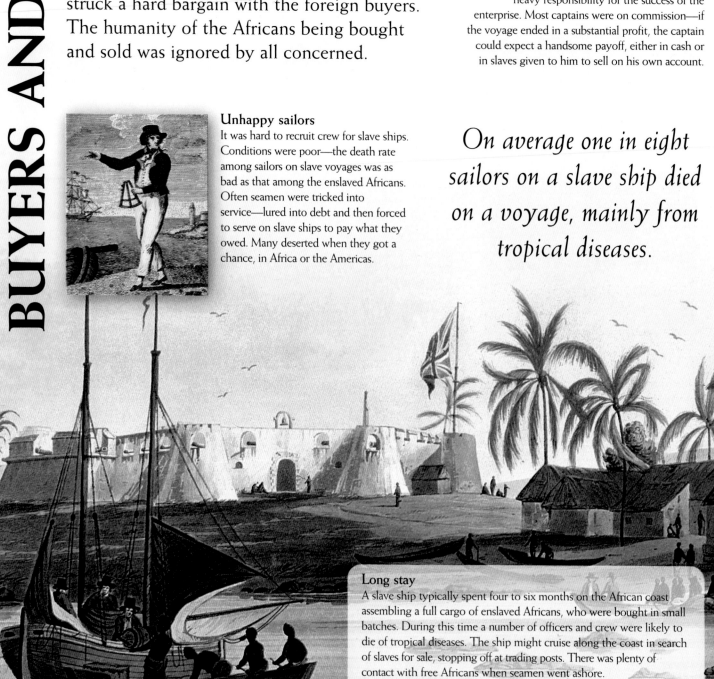

Long stay
A slave ship typically spent four to six months on the African coast assembling a full cargo of enslaved Africans, who were bought in small batches. During this time a number of officers and crew were likely to die of tropical diseases. The ship might cruise along the coast in search of slaves for sale, stopping off at trading posts. There was plenty of contact with free Africans when seamen went ashore.

Factor on the coast

Some European merchants established "factories" on the African coast—buildings where their agents or factors could live and where slaves were held before being taken on board ship. The factor's tasks included ensuring that any taxes levied by the local ruler on the export of slaves were paid, and establishing a relationship of trust with African traders.

Branded humans

Once purchased, enslaved Africans were branded with the mark of the merchant who had paid for them, as if they were cattle. Their heads were shaved and their clothes taken— supposedly to prevent the spread of disease, but perhaps also as a humiliation for the captives. Many died while still on the African coast, waiting months for shipment across the Atlantic.

Buying people

Buying slaves was a degrading business. Europeans examined the enslaved people physically, as if they were animals, to see if they were healthy. Fit men with a long working life ahead of them were most wanted. Twice as many men as women were taken.

"Is it not strange to think, that they who ought to be considered as the most learned and civilized people in the world, that they should carry on a traffic of the most barbarous cruelty and injustice, and that many... are become so dissolute as to think slavery, robbery, and murder no crime...?"

Former slave Ottobah Cugoano, Narrative of the Enslavement of a Native of Africa, *1787*

A caravan of slaves in the African interior in 1795

THE MIDDLE PASSAGE

KNOWN AS THE "MIDDLE PASSAGE," the crossing of the Atlantic from West Africa to the Caribbean or the American mainland usually took around six weeks. Such a voyage was fraught with dangers and hardships, since the ships were threatened by storms, shortages of food and water, and outbreaks of disease. On a slaving ship it was a nightmare journey for the human cargo. They were imprisoned below decks in filthy, overcrowded conditions, subject to brutal treatment by the crew. Captains had a financial interest in keeping their valuable human cargo alive and in good condition, but deaths were commonplace. Bodies were thrown overboard to feed the sharks that tracked the ships across the ocean.

Crowded conditions
Enslaved Africans were packed into the confined space of the ship's lower decks. Male slaves were often chained together in pairs, although women and children were usually not shackled. The ceilings were so low there was not even room to stand up. This model represents the tightly packed 18th-century slave ship *Brookes*.

Brookes *slave ship was built to carry 451 slaves but often had more than 600 slaves on board.*

Stormy weather
Slave ships had ventilation holes to allow air into the overcrowded holds, but when ships hit rough seas all openings had to be closed. Conditions below deck then became even more appalling, with captives packed together without air or light, many of them violently seasick.

"Dancing" on deck

Slaves were valuable property, and needed to be kept alive and healthy, so it was customary to force them to exercise on deck every day. They were made to dance, often wearing their shackles, while the crew looked on. This was humiliating for the prisoners, but any who refused to dance were flogged.

Food and drink

On board slaves were typically fed beans, rice, yams, and salted pork or beef. Carrying enough food and water for some 600 captives and a ship's crew was difficult. If the ship made a slow crossing, thirst and hunger would set in.

Outbreak of disease

The greatest killer on a voyage was disease. Many of the enslaved Africans contracted the "flux," or dysentery, a disease caused by poor-quality drinking water. Dysentery made conditions especially foul below decks. Scurvy, caused by a lack of fresh fruit and vegetables, was another common ailment. Most slave ships employed a ship's surgeon or doctor, but at that time few diseases could be cured.

Lack of supplies

Shortages of drinking water and food compelled some captains to take drastic measures to save their cargo. In 1781, Luke Collingwood, the captain of the slave ship *Zong*, with dwindling water supplies and a rapidly sickening cargo, ordered his crew to throw 133 sick but living Africans overboard. The ship's owners then filed an insurance claim to cover the loss.

VOICES THE CROSSING

Millions of enslaved Africans experienced the horrors of the "Middle Passage" aboard slave ships crossing the Atlantic. Today, we can scarcely imagine their sufferings. Only a few snatches of testimony have survived from the enslaved Africans themselves, but along with accounts written by slave traders and officers running the ships, they give us a vivid and detailed picture of the hellish conditions.

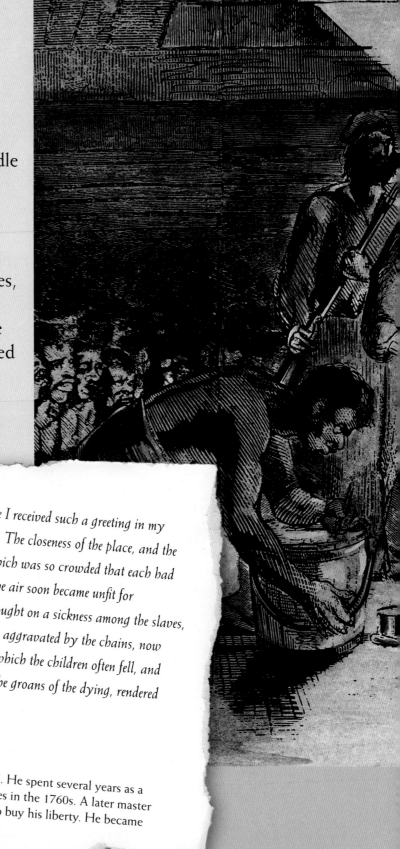

"*I WAS SOON put down under the decks, and there I received such a greeting in my nostrils as I had never experienced in my life... The closeness of the place, and the heat of the climate, added to the number in the ship, which was so crowded that each had scarcely room to turn himself, almost suffocated us. The air soon became unfit for respiration, from a variety of loathsome smells, and brought on a sickness among the slaves, of which many died. The wretched situation was again aggravated by the chains, now unsupportable, and the filth of the necessary tubs, into which the children often fell, and were almost suffocated. The shrieks of the women, and the groans of the dying, rendered the whole a scene of horror almost inconceivable.*"

Olaudah Equiano was born in Essaka, Nigeria, in 1745. He spent several years as a slave in Africa before he was shipped to the West Indies in the 1760s. A later master let him earn money on his own behalf, enabling him to buy his liberty. He became important as a campaigner against the slave trade.

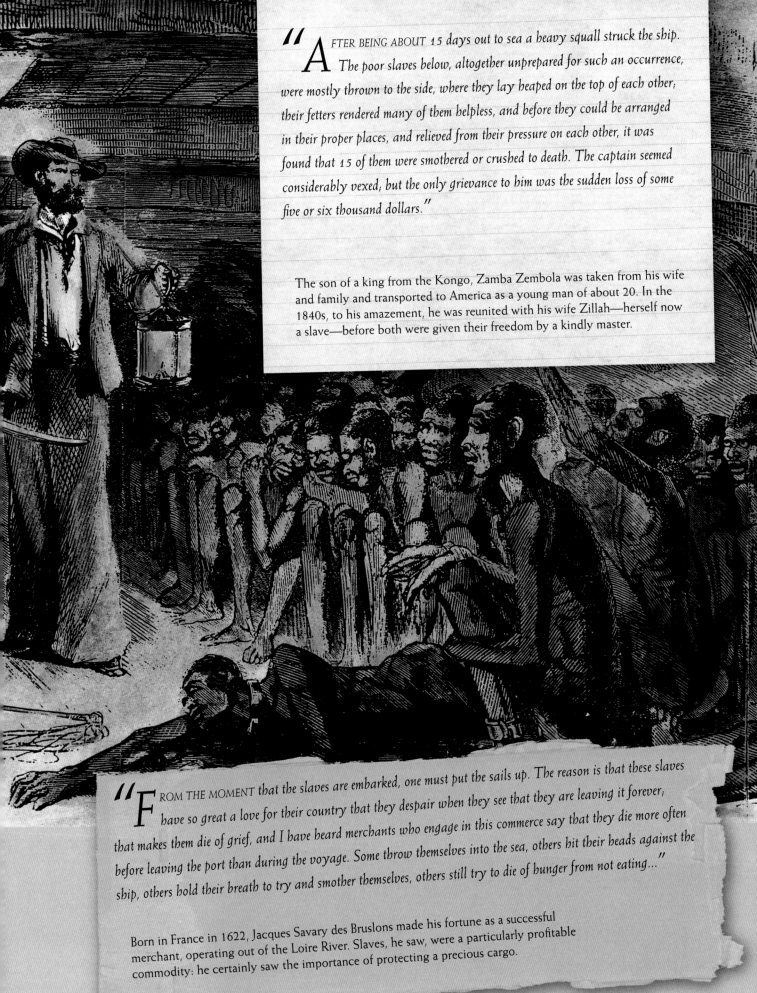

"AFTER BEING ABOUT 15 days out to sea a heavy squall struck the ship. The poor slaves below, altogether unprepared for such an occurrence, were mostly thrown to the side, where they lay heaped on the top of each other; their fetters rendered many of them helpless, and before they could be arranged in their proper places, and relieved from their pressure on each other, it was found that 15 of them were smothered or crushed to death. The captain seemed considerably vexed; but the only grievance to him was the sudden loss of some five or six thousand dollars."

The son of a king from the Kongo, Zamba Zembola was taken from his wife and family and transported to America as a young man of about 20. In the 1840s, to his amazement, he was reunited with his wife Zillah—herself now a slave—before both were given their freedom by a kindly master.

"FROM THE MOMENT that the slaves are embarked, one must put the sails up. The reason is that these slaves have so great a love for their country that they despair when they see that they are leaving it forever; that makes them die of grief, and I have heard merchants who engage in this commerce say that they die more often before leaving the port than during the voyage. Some throw themselves into the sea, others hit their heads against the ship, others hold their breath to try and smother themselves, others still try to die of hunger from not eating..."

Born in France in 1622, Jacques Savary des Bruslons made his fortune as a successful merchant, operating out of the Loire River. Slaves, he saw, were a particularly profitable commodity: he certainly saw the importance of protecting a precious cargo.

INSURRECTION AND RESISTANCE

Armed crews

Slave ships carried far more sailors than an ordinary merchant ship, because of the need to control the captives in the hold. Even so, the crew was heavily outnumbered by the slaves. The sailors were understandably very afraid of these captives, who had every reason to hate their captors. Enslaved men were kept shackled, though the women and children were given more freedom on the voyage. Sailors always had guns and cutlasses (above) in preparation for any slave uprising.

ENSLAVED AFRICANS resisted transportation across the ocean with acts of individual defiance and collective insurrection, or open revolt. To launch a full-scale insurrection the men needed to free themselves from their shackles, aided by the women or child captives who were left unchained. Once loose, the men would try to overwhelm the crew by force of numbers. Sadly, even if they succeeded in seizing control, they were unlikely to know how to sail the ship.

Self-destruction

The most direct form of resistance available to an enslaved person was suicide. There were many cases of slaves deliberately jumping overboard or refusing food until they starved to death. Self-starvation was so common that slave ships carried a speculum oris, a crude device used to force-feed any slaves who would not eat.

Brutal captains

The captain of a slave ship had absolute power over his little realm during the voyage. Some captains were as reasonably behaved as was possible in such a brutal situation, but others were sadists and tyrants who made their ships a living hell. They repeatedly flogged and tortured both slaves and crew in a reign of terror.

It is estimated there were revolts on ten in every 100 slave voyages.

Cruel punishments

After a failed insurrection, those slaves responsible were subjected to extreme punishments. Flogging was common. Afterward substances were rubbed into the wounds to increase the victim's pain. Another form of torture was the thumbscrew, tightened until it crushed a finger.

Revolt aboard

Insurrections were commonplace. Historians estimate that about ten percent of slave ships experienced insurrections significant enough to produce at least one death. This painting shows the insurrection on board the *Amistad*, while it was transporting 53 captives from Havana in Cuba in 1839. The captives violently attacked their crew before taking control of the ship. But instead of sailing back to Africa, they ended up in Long Island, New York.

Solidarity

It was hard for all the enslaved Africans in a hold to cooperate because they usually belonged to different ethnic groups. These groups might be traditional enemies, and in any case could not understand one another's languages. But bonds of friendship and trust did develop between captives on their dreadful journey. Africans in the Caribbean used the term "shipmates" for people who had endured the Atlantic crossing on the same ship as they had.

"We stood in arms, firing on the revolted slaves, of whom we killed some… and many of the most mutinous leaped over board, and drowned themselves in the ocean with much resolution, showing no manner of concern for life."

James Barbot, sailor, describes an insurrection on the British slave ship Don Carlos, *1732*

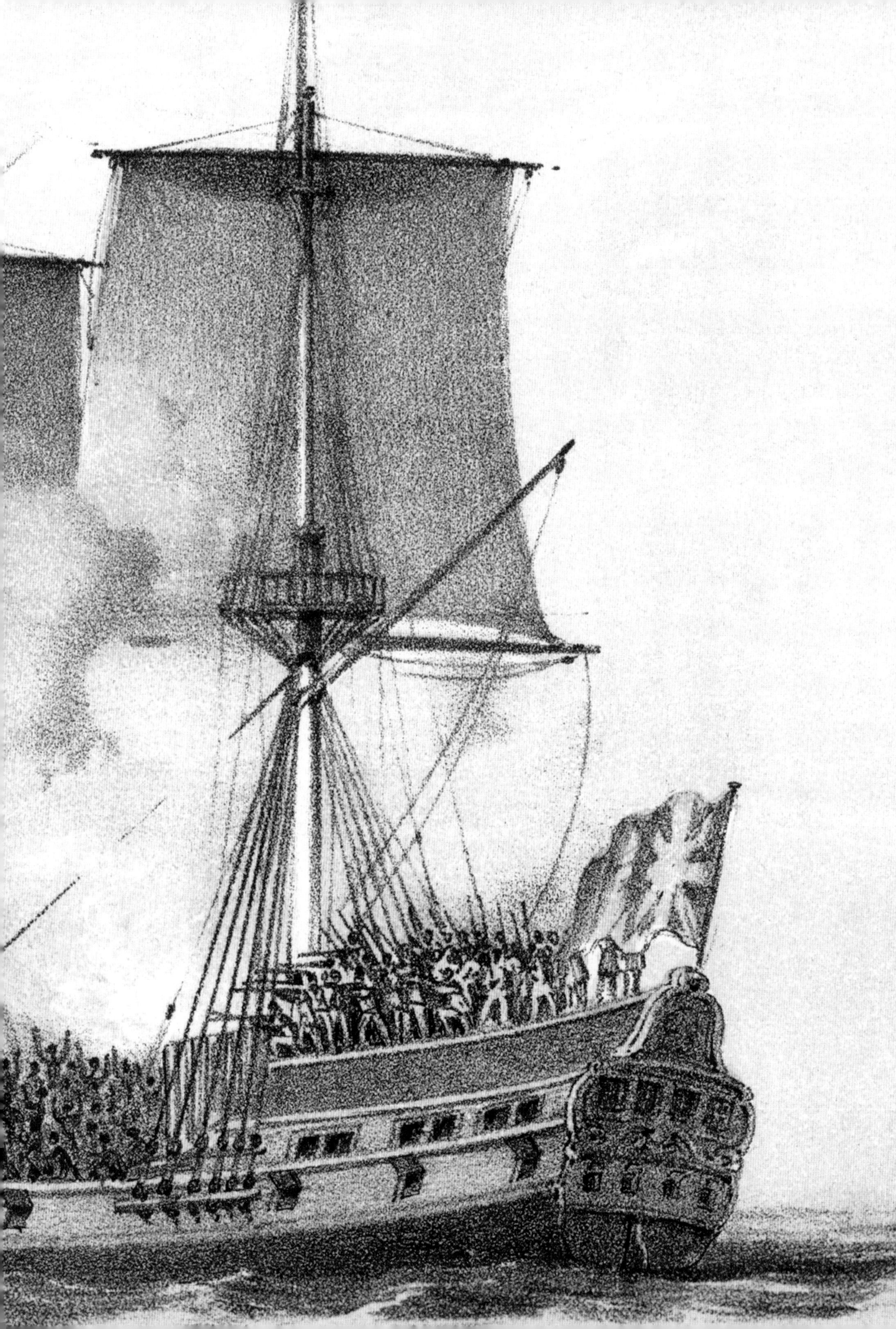

Insurrection on a slave ship, by W. L. Walton, 1851

ARRIVAL AND SALE

THEIR ARRIVAL IN THE NEW WORLD was the start of fresh sufferings for enslaved Africans. Offered for sale in port, the enslaved had no control over how they were disposed of. Those who up to that point had managed to stay together with relatives from home, or had formed friendships on board ship, were now ruthlessly split apart from family and comrades, and sold to different owners. Large numbers of men, women, and children who had survived the ocean crossing died in the early months after arrival in the Americas, unable to cope either with unfamiliar diseases or with the shock of being put to work on a plantation.

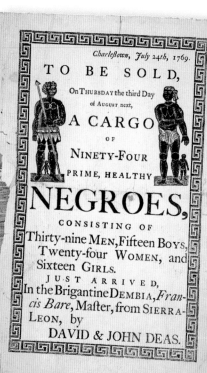

Charlestown, July 24th, 1769.
TO BE SOLD,
On THURSDAY the third Day
of AUGUST next,
A CARGO
OF
NINETY-FOUR
PRIME, HEALTHY
NEGROES,
CONSISTING OF
Thirty-nine MEN, Fifteen BOYS,
Twenty-four WOMEN, and
Sixteen GIRLS.
JUST ARRIVED,
In the Brigantine DEMBIA, Francis Bare, Master, from SIERRA-LEON, by
DAVID & JOHN DEAS.

Coming ashore
Traders wanted to make their captives look healthy to fetch a good price. Before landing, they were given better food for several days so they looked "refreshed." Their bodies were rubbed with palm oils to make them appear in better physical condition.

Advertised for sale
New arrivals were advertised by posters. Young men generally commanded the highest prices. Some buyers preferred slaves from particular African regions. This poster emphasizes that the slaves for sale are from Sierra Leone—they were valued in Carolina for their rice-farming skills.

Selling methods
Enslaved people were often sold on deck or at the dockside. Buyers from the plantations visited the slave ship in port, and took their pick of the new arrivals. Another method of sale was a "scramble sale," in which purchasers grabbed what slaves they could in a chaotic free-for-all.

Restocking the ship
After arriving in the Americas, the captain of the slave ship was occupied with loading up with goods for the voyage home—typically a plantation product such as sugar or tobacco.

As many as one in 20 slaves who reached the New World died before they could be sold.

Sold at auction
Slave-importing towns had an auction block at which the enslaved were put up for sale. Prices would go up and down depending on supply and demand. The depressed state and poor condition of the Africans were usually only too obvious. This illustration shows a slave auction in the streets of New Amsterdam—the future New York—organized by Dutch traders in 1655.

Careful buyers
Being subjected to close physical examination was one of the humiliations visited upon the enslaved throughout the history of slavery. If slaves were in short supply, buyers would take almost any on offer. But when they were in a position to choose, they carefully selected those Africans they thought healthiest and most suitable for hard work.

LIFE IN SLAVERY

THE ATLANTIC SLAVE TRADE created a vast population of African origin in the Americas. Although some eventually gained their freedom, the majority remained enslaved, providing most of the workforce for the continent's economic development from the 1600s to the 1800s. At first, all black Americans were African-born, but over time increasing numbers were born in the Americas. These people gradually forged a distinctive African-American identity.

Valuable harvest
Enslaved men and women cut the sugar cane using machetes, then loaded it onto carts to be taken to the mill for processing. The sugar was exported around the world, making plantation owners rich.

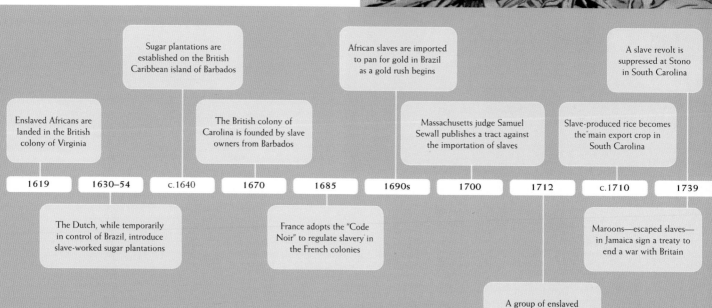

Sugar plantations are established on the British Caribbean island of Barbados

African slaves are imported to pan for gold in Brazil as a gold rush begins

A slave revolt is suppressed at Stono in South Carolina

Enslaved Africans are landed in the British colony of Virginia

The British colony of Carolina is founded by slave owners from Barbados

Massachusetts judge Samuel Sewall publishes a tract against the importation of slaves

Slave-produced rice becomes the main export crop in South Carolina

| 1619 | 1630–54 | c.1640 | 1670 | 1685 | 1690s | 1700 | 1712 | c.1710 | 1739 |

The Dutch, while temporarily in control of Brazil, introduce slave-worked sugar plantations

France adopts the "Code Noir" to regulate slavery in the French colonies

Maroons—escaped slaves—in Jamaica sign a treaty to end a war with Britain

A group of enslaved Africans in New York rebel, killing nine white people

Thirteen former British
colonies declare their
independence

The Free African Society is
founded by free people of
color in Philadelphia

The number of enslaved
people in the US
reaches nearly 1 million

Slavery is authorized
in the colony of
Georgia

Vermont is the first state in
the US to abolish slavery

The African Methodist
Episcopal Church is
founded in Philadelphia

About 75 percent of
US slaves work in the
cotton industry

| 1750 | 1760s | 1776 | 1777 | 1787 | 1794 | 1800 | 1808 | 1850s | 1860 |

The French Caribbean colony of
Saint-Domingue (Haiti) becomes
a major source of sugar

Eli Whitney invents the cotton gin,
leading to a massive expansion of
cotton growing in the Southern US

The US ceases
importing slaves
from Africa

The number of enslaved
people in the US reaches
about 4 million

The First African Baptist
Church is founded by
George Liele in Georgia

Slave population in the US c.1830

Regions with significant slave population

Major crops grown in the United States

◇ cotton   ⦨ rice

⌇ tobacco   ⚱ sugar

⊛ indigo

Slaves in North America

The distribution of enslaved people corresponded largely to the distribution of crops. Most slaves were found where crops such as sugar, tobacco, coffee, cocoa, indigo (a dye stuff), and later cotton were worked on plantations.

Caribbean islands

The islands of the Caribbean were European colonies. Devoted mostly to plantation agriculture, they became slave societies, that is, societies in which the majority of the population were enslaved people or freed slaves.

WHERE ENSLAVED PEOPLE LIVED

ENSLAVED PEOPLE OF AFRICAN ORIGIN were to be found wherever Europeans extended their rule in the New World. However, the vast majority ended up in the sugar-producing colonies of Brazil and the Caribbean. Only four percent ended up in mainland North America, what is today the United States. An enslaved person's life chances depended on where they lived. Early deaths were more common in Brazil and the Caribbean than in the United States because of the torrid climate and the rigors of year-round sugar production.

Brazilian majority

The largest enslaved population in the Americas was in Brazil. In 1800, about two-thirds of the population of Brazil was of African origin. Enslaved Africans continued to be imported to Brazil, until the government abolished the slave trade in 1850.

Enslaved Americans

The North American colonies, which became the United States in 1776, had a relatively small enslaved population until the 1800s. While Africans made up more than 90 percent of the population in places like Jamaica, North America had a white majority, even in the South. The only states that developed a black majority were South Carolina, by the start of the 1700s, and Mississippi, by the mid-1800s. In the first half of the 1800s, the enslaved population of the South grew from about 700,000 to 4 million—but this was still slower than the growth among white Americans.

Freed slaves

In Brazil, many enslaved people were freed by their owners and others escaped to rebel "maroon societies." It was also usual for the child of a slave owner and slave woman to be granted freedom. By 1800, a quarter of all people of African descent in Brazil were free. Here, finely dressed Brazilian free people of color serve refreshments in Rio de Janeiro.

WHAT SLAVES DID

THE LABOR OF THE ENSLAVED was central to the economic development of the Americas. Most enslaved people worked on plantations, but many did other jobs. Some were mule drivers or carters who traveled on their master's business. Some worked as sailors or dockers, or were skilled artisans or personal servants. Some made money selling food in markets or making furniture.

Tobacco workers
In 18th-century Virginia, tobacco was the main slave-grown crop. Produced on small farms and large estates, it did not demand such laborious year-round toil as sugar cane. But caring for the tobacco plants (right) and curing the harvested leaves required skill as well as hard work. If slaves had time left over, they grew corn or tended animals.

Enslaved in the city
Considerable numbers of enslaved people lived in towns and cities. The life of urban slaves was different from that of slaves on a plantation. They were generally less closely supervised, but they were still subject to bad treatment and could be sold at any time.

Gold and diamonds

In places such as the Minas Gerais region of Brazil, enslaved workers were used to pan for gold and diamonds in fast-flowing streams and rivers. This was exceptionally tough work. Sifting for gold all year round in cold water brought frequent illness and a shockingly high death rate.

From the age of eight, children worked in the fields or in other jobs.

Domestic staff

Many of the enslaved, especially women, worked as domestic servants in white households, cleaning, cooking, and looking after children. This Brazilian government official strides ahead of his family and his domestic slaves.

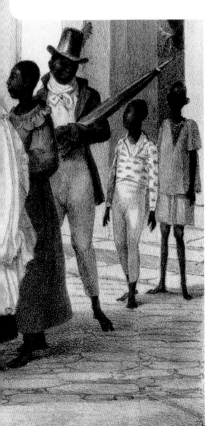

Rice plantation

The major slave-produced crop in coastal South Carolina was rice. The enslaved changed their tasks with the seasons, which allowed them to take much greater control of their working lives. Working barefoot in the fields, the enslaved sowed rice in spring and harvested it in September. There was no rest in the winter, since tasks included threshing grain and repairing irrigation works.

Personal servants

Some male slaves became trusted servants to their masters, who might even take them along on wide-ranging travels. This black servant is being dressed up for a special occasion by his owner's daughter.

SUGAR PLANTATIONS

WORKING ON SUGAR PLANTATIONS in the West Indies or Brazil was probably the hardest life an enslaved person could face. Every year, thousands were literally worked to death. The slaves not only had to plant and cut the sugar cane, but also toil in sugar mills on the plantation, processing the cane into sugar. At the height of the harvesting season, enslaved men and women would be working by day in the fields and by night in the mill, with little time to eat or sleep. This relentless labor, done under the threat of the whip, generated large profits for plantation owners.

In the fields
Throughout the year, the workers had to dig trenches to plant the cane shoots, weed and manure the ground for the growing plants, and then cut the cane. All these tasks involved backbreaking labor, but the slaves had no time to rest. Work in the cane fields was supervised by slave drivers with whips.

Work in the sugar mill
The harvested sugar cane had to be crushed through rollers and the extract boiled in cauldrons. Cane waste was used to feed the furnaces. Conditions for those working in the sugar mill were hard and dangerous. The heat was intense. It was easy for an exhausted person to make a mistake and lose an arm by getting it trapped in the crushing rollers.

The average life expectancy of an enslaved African imported to work on a sugar plantation was about six years.

Living space
The enslaved workers typically lived in simple huts. They were expected to feed themselves, growing food crops such as yams and beans on land not needed for sugar cane.

Owners and overseers
The white owners, agents, and overseers who ran sugar plantations were heavily outnumbered. There might only be a couple of white people on a plantation with a hundred slaves. Fearing a revolt, they used harsh discipline as intimidation.

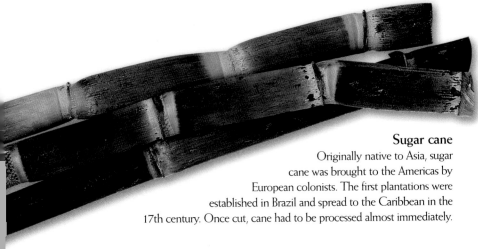

Sugar cane
Originally native to Asia, sugar cane was brought to the Americas by European colonists. The first plantations were established in Brazil and spread to the Caribbean in the 17th century. Once cut, cane had to be processed almost immediately.

MOLASSES AND RUM
Rum, an alcoholic beverage, was made from molasses, a by-product of sugar cane processing. Trade in molasses and rum became an important element in the slave system, especially from the point of view of the North American colonies. Rum production, using molasses extracted from the cane grown on Caribbean slave plantations, was big business in 18th-century New England.

VOICES FORCED LABOR

Many West Indian sugar plantations in the 17th and 18th centuries were run like prison camps. Enslaved people were subjected to a reign of terror. Any sign of resistance was met with savage punishment. Slave owners allowed the enslaved to die of maltreatment and overwork, knowing they could be replaced by new purchases from Africa.

"BEING IN THIS dreadful captivity and horrible slavery, without any hope of deliverance, for about eight or nine months, beholding the most dreadful scenes of misery and cruelty, and seeing my miserable companions often cruelly lashed, and, as it were, cut to pieces, for the most trifling faults; this made me often tremble and weep... For eating a piece of sugar cane, some were cruelly lashed, or struck over the face, to knock their teeth out... Some told me they had their teeth pulled out, to deter others, and to prevent them from eating any cane in future... I may safely say, that all the poverty and misery that any of the inhabitants of Africa meet with among themselves, is far inferior to those inhospitable regions of misery which they meet with in the West Indies..."

Ottobah Cugoano, kidnapped as a youth in West Africa, was transported to Grenada in the West Indies, where he worked for nine months on a sugar plantation in the 1760s. He survived and, in 1787 in Britain, published his *Narrative of the Enslavement of Ottobah Cugoano, a Native of Africa.*

"THE NEGROES WHO were all in troops are sorted so as to match each other in size and strength. Every ten negroes have a driver, who walks behind them, holding in his hand a short whip and a long one. You will easily guess the use of these weapons; a circumstance of all others the most horrid. They are naked, male and female down to the girdle [waist], and you constantly observe where application [of the whip] has been made."

Englishwoman Janet Schaw visited the Caribbean islands of Antigua and St. Christopher in the 1770s, as the guest of sugar-plantation owners. Despite her initial shock at the sufferings of the enslaved, she found that "the horror of it must wear off," convincing herself that Africans were less capable of suffering than Europeans.

"THE PUNISHMENTS FOR crimes of slaves are usually, for rebellions, burning them by nailing them down on the ground with crooked sticks on every limb, and applying the fire by degrees from the feet and hands, burning them gradually up to the head, whereby their pains are extravagant... For negligence they are usually whipped by the overseers with hardwood switches, till they be all bloody. After they are whipped till they are raw, some put on their skins pepper and salt to make them smart..."

Hans Sloane (1660–1753), the Irish-born founder of the British Museum, was a learned doctor and president of the Royal Society. He accompanied his firsthand observations on punishments on West Indian plantations with the comment that these were "sometimes merited by the slaves" and only "appeared harsh."

Slavery in New York
The first colony in North America to have a large enslaved population was New York. By 1770, there were more enslaved blacks there than in the Southern colony of Georgia. Many enslaved people worked on the Manhattan waterfront.

Doubts about enslavement
Some white Americans were not happy about importing enslaved Africans. The Massachusetts judge and successful merchant Samuel Sewall published *The Selling of Joseph*, the first pamphlet opposing the importing of slaves, in 1700.

SLAVES OF THE COLONISTS

IN THE NORTH AMERICAN COLONIES that in 1776 became the United States, a slave system was slower to develop than in the Caribbean or Brazil. Many more white people worked in North America under systems of forced labor. Nonetheless, enslaved Africans became a commonplace feature of life in North American towns and countryside during the 1600s and 1700s. Black people faced a barrier of racism as well as enslavement, and laws deprived free African-Americans of the same rights as whites.

Deep South
Cotton became the main slave-produced crop in North America in the early 1800s. In the decades that followed, the cotton fields of the Deep South—inland Georgia and Carolina, Alabama, Louisiana, Mississippi, and Texas—became the new focus of slave labor.

In South Carolina, it was a crime to teach a slave to read and write.

DATE	ENSLAVED POPULATION OF NORTH AMERICA
1700	28,000
1770	460,000
1800	894,000
1860	4,000,000

Natural growth

Although they were no better treated than enslaved people elsewhere in the Americas, slaves in North America had a better chance of survival because the supply of food was more plentiful and there were fewer deadly diseases. Some 400,000 Africans were forcibly imported and the enslaved population grew rapidly through natural increase—more births than deaths—from the late 18th century.

Tobacco workers

The largest numbers of slaves in the North American colonies before independence were in Virginia and Maryland. Two out of every five Virginians were enslaved. The Africans were originally imported to work on tobacco farms. By the late 1700s, slaves were increasingly used in growing corn or in mines and manufacturing jobs.

Port of Charleston

The Carolina colony was founded by slave owners from the island of Barbados. The Carolina port of Charleston served as the main point of entry for enslaved Africans into North America. Charleston became a thriving centre of African-American life in the 1700s, with black artisans and market traders flourishing.

AFRICAN BURIAL GROUND

In 1991, a 200-year-old cemetery of free and enslaved African-Americans was uncovered by construction workers in Lower Manhattan, New York. Remains of more than 400 people who died between 1690 and 1790 were found in coffins, many of them children. The Burial Ground is now a National Monument for the public to visit.

RESISTING BONDAGE

ENSLAVED PEOPLE naturally resented mistreatment and longed for freedom. There were some large-scale slave revolts, especially on Caribbean islands where the majority of the population was black. In some places, runaway slaves formed fiercely independent rebel communities that defended themselves against the white authorities. In North America, it was harder for runaways to find a refuge and revolt was doomed to fail, but the enslaved practiced passive resistance—going on a strike or working at a slow pace—and individual acts of disobedience.

Fugitive war
Escaped slaves controlled large areas of the British-owned island of Jamaica, Dutch-ruled Surinam, and Brazil. The runaways, or fugitives, were skillful fighters who waged war on forces sent to suppress them. In Surinam, the authorities armed blacks to fight against the fugitive bands, rewarding them with freedom. This black ranger was painted by artist William Blake in 1806.

Hunting runaways
Running away was a hard decision to make, since it meant not only taking a huge risk, but also leaving family and friends. Slave owners did all they could to track down fugitives, since they considered slaves their valuable property.

Uprising in the North

North American slave revolts were infrequent because the whites were too powerful. In 1739, for example, at the Stono River, South Carolina, a group of 80 slaves seized firearms and marched toward freedom in Spanish-owned Florida. All were hunted down and killed. Similarly, when Nat Turner led a bloody uprising in Virginia in 1831, left, it was brutally suppressed within two days.

In 1739, the British signed a treaty with fugitive slaves— the Maroons—in Jamaica, allowing them to rule parts of the island.

Douglass and the slave breaker

Frederick Douglass, an enslaved person who became a leader of the movement for the abolition of slavery in the United States, had bitter experience of punishment. Aged 16, he was sent by his owner to a farmer who had a reputation for "breaking" independent-minded slaves. Douglass was whipped frequently, but refused to be broken. He escaped at the age of 20 by catching a train dressed in a sailor's uniform.

Brutal punishments

Disobedience and escape were discouraged by cruel punishments. These extended from whipping and being tied up to physical mutilation— the cutting off of ears or, in extreme cases, amputation of hands or limbs. Sometimes enslaved persons were made to wear iron masks or neck collars as a punishment for insubordination. Factories made a good profit manufacturing such items.

"Fifty lashes were laid on before stopping… While I suffered under this dreadful torture, I prayed, and wept, and implored mercy at the hand of slavery, but found none."

Henry Bibb, born into slavery on a Kentucky plantation in 1815, describes his punishment for attempting to escape

A slave is punished by his overseer in an illustration from 1835

SLAVE FAMILIES

IN THE UNITED STATES, the enslaved were no freer in their personal relationships and family lives than in any other aspect of existence. Marriages between enslaved people were not legally recognized by white society and were subject to the will of owners. Slave husbands, wives, and children could be cruelly separated at any time by sale, or by the owner's change in fortune or death. Yet slaves did manage to create solid family bonds against all odds.

Conflict of authority

Slave owners liked to pose as paternal to their slaves and did not like any resistance to their absolute authority. This made it especially hard for slave fathers to exercise any authority of their own over their children or to protect them against the owner. Having to watch while another family member was mistreated was a cruel experience.

Reared in slavery

Children born on a large plantation might have the good fortune to grow up with their parents and wider family, with everyone employed in the same place. But all too often, children were brought up by mothers alone, their father having been sold elsewhere. About one in ten enslaved children in the United States grew up with neither parent.

Faithful spouses

Most of the enslaved succeeded in forming long relationships, even though about one-in-four slave marriages was split by the sale of one spouse. Couples often lived and worked on different plantations. Owners often granted visiting rights, allowing spouses to meet, or men to see their children.

Overworked women
The hard labor imposed on slave women made it difficult for them to care for their children. Mothers carried babies while working in the fields, but older children might be left unsupervised all day. Here, a small child is greeted by the slave-owner's wife.

Quest for a son
The story of Sojourner Truth, who later became a famous abolitionist, illustrates the harshness of family life under slavery. Her owner forced her to marry an older slave against her will. After gaining freedom in New York, she had to battle to recover her son, Peter, who had been sold at the age of five in distant Alabama.

Many enslaved children were taken from their mothers and sold while still babies.

Extended family
The enslaved determinedly built up family links, maintaining bonds of kinship across wide geographical areas. People sold to new owners might find relatives in their new homes. The enslaved also created "family" relationships with people who had no blood relationship to them.

SLAVE OWNERS

SLAVE OWNERS were a diverse body of people. Many were immensely wealthy and owned substantial land. But people who were far from rich might also own a few slaves. Almost all owners were white, though in some rare cases slaves might be owned by free black people or even Native Americans. Many owners used their power with extreme cruelty; others showed humanity as far as the situation allowed.

Idle rich
Many Caribbean plantations belonged to wealthy absentee landowners in Europe, whose plantations were looked after by overseers or estate managers. Plantation owners who lived in the West Indies mostly enjoyed idle lives, and were waited upon by their slaves.

Paternal attitudes
Many slave owners saw themselves as caring father-figures who "looked after" their slave "family." In an attempt to be treated better, the enslaved would often play up to the slave-owners' wish to be loved and admired. This Virginia plantation owner is visiting the slaves on his estate.

Slave-owning rebel
Henry Laurens of South Carolina made a fortune as a slave trader, and invested his money in a plantation. When the American colonies revolted against British rule in 1775, Laurens was a leading rebel. Although he said he hated slavery, he would not free his own slaves.

Twelve American presidents were slave owners—the last president to own slaves was Ulysses S. Grant.

George Washington, the slave owner
Some people were born into the slave-holding class. The first United States President, George Washington, inherited slaves at the age of 10. Unlike most masters, he refused to break up slave families by selling individuals and he made provision in his will to free all his slaves.

Brazilian inequality
In Brazil, there was a less absolute division between the races than in the United States—and there tended to be more social contact between different races. But on a plantation it was still the enslaved who worked and the white man who watched.

KING COTTON

IT TAKES AN ENORMOUS AMOUNT of hard work to turn raw cotton into usable fabric, but it was well worth it as far as America's planters were concerned. The crop became known as "King Cotton," since it became the mainstay of the Southern economy. Many factories, banks, railroads, and merchant houses of the Northern states depended on it, too. It was the slaves who underpinned all this. In 1790, the United States produced about 1.5 million pounds (680,000 kg) of raw cotton; by 1860, output stood at almost 2.2 billion pounds (1 billion kg) a year.

About 75 percent of America's slaves were involved in cotton production in the 1850s.

Fiber facts
The cloth we call cotton starts as the cushiony mass of white fibers (or staples) protecting the seeds inside the seed-pod (or boll) of the cotton plant. The fibers have to be separated from the seeds themselves before they can be used. Individually, they are soft but strong, and although they look straight they are spiral in form, so they bond together well when spun into a yarn.

Planting season
March and April were planting times. One slave drove a mule-drawn plow, breaking up the soil. A second slave followed and sowed seeds in the furrow the first had made. A third used another mule-drawn plow to cover it over. Constant hoeing was needed in the months that followed to destroy weeds and make sure the cotton bushes were neatly spaced.

Extended harvest

The bolls ripened gradually, so picking went on from August to January—five months of unrelenting labor for slaves, both men and women. They carried enormous bags strapped around their necks. Stooping, they plucked the cotton, working gradually along the rows to the ends where giant wicker baskets waited to be filled. The bags were weighed before emptying, so each slave's output—on average, about 150 pounds (68 kg) a day—could be tracked.

Hard labor

Cotton-picking was grueling labor, which made every muscle ache, and slaves were forced to work by frequent floggings. Slaves seen idling were savagely whipped. One or more strokes of the whip would be given for every pound a slave fell short of his or her target.

BARREN LAND

America's plantations achieved yields of up to 1,500 pounds (680 kg) per acre (0.4 hectare), but that productivity came at a heavy price. It was not just slaves who were worked to death; the soil itself was exhausted by the endless demands the growing cotton made on the earth for minerals. As early as the 1830s, large tracts of eastern Georgia had been left barren, forcing the westward expansion of the cotton-growing area.

Cotton machine

Ironically, it was a labor-saving device that made large-scale cotton production in America possible, ensuring a life of toil for generations of slaves. Eli Whitney's cotton gin (short for "engine"), invented in 1793, drew the cotton through spiked rollers, separating the staples from the seeds. With Whitney's gin, one slave could process 50 times more cotton a day than with the earlier hand-rollers.

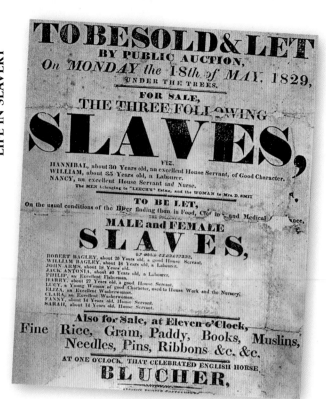

For sale or rent
Slaves were valuable property and an auctioneer might consider it worth printing a poster to advertise the sale of just three of them. The enslaved were also "let"—that is, rented out to employers who had a use for their labor.

SOLD AND MOVED

ENSLAVED PEOPLE had no control over their own lives and could be sold and moved without warning. This insecurity was one of the most resented features of the enslaved condition. A sale might happen when an owner died or went bankrupt, or for financial gain. In Virginia by the 1800s, slaves were more valuable to an owner as breeders of children for sale than as workers.

In 1860, the estimated value of America's 4 million slaves was $4 billion.

Auction houses
Enslaved people were auctioned like any other property. Before the bidding began, they were paraded in front of potential buyers, subjected to physical examination, and interrogated about their skills. They were then exhibited for public sale in the auction room.

Going South

In the 1800s, the United States developed a large-scale internal slave trade, as slaves living in the eastern states were sold and moved to the cotton fields of the Deep South. British artist Eyre Crowe witnessed these slaves being transported from Richmond, Virginia, in 1853.

Tearing apart families

Young children were among those for sale at auction. They were often sold apart from their parents, giving rise to heartbreaking scenes of separation. This illustration is from the antislavery novel *Uncle Tom's Cabin* by Harriet Beecher Stowe (1852).

Image of suffering

The moment of cruel separation when a mother was split from her child, or husband from wife, was often depicted by campaigners against slavery. This image is from an 1860s' print called: *The Parting: "Buy Us Too."*

Herded in chains

To feed the demand for labor in the cotton fields, slave traders moved tens of thousands of slaves by boat around the coast of the United States to New Orleans or overland on foot. Columns of shackled slaves, threatened by whips, made painful progress.

VOICES
TREATED LIKE ANIMALS

The experience of being sold at auction like farm animals was a gross humiliation for enslaved people. The emotional distress it caused was frequently multiplied by separation from loved ones as families were torn apart, with husbands, wives, and children sold to different people. Slave owners often used the threat of sale as a way of disciplining their enslaved workforce.

"*AT LENGTH THE vendue [auction] master, who was to offer us for sale like sheep or cattle, arrived, and asked my mother which was the eldest. She said nothing, but pointed to me… I was soon surrounded by strange men, who examined and handled me in the same manner that a butcher would a calf or a lamb he was about to purchase, and who talked about my shape and size in like words—as if I could no more understand their meaning than the dumb beasts. I was then put up to sale. The bidding commenced at a few pounds, and gradually rose to fifty-seven… and the people who stood by said that I had fetched a great sum for so young a slave.*"

Mary Prince was born into slavery in Bermuda in about 1788. She was sold apart from her mother and sisters at the age of ten. She later became a prominent campaigner for the abolition of slavery, publishing her autobiography, *The History of Mary Prince, a West Indian Slave*, in 1831.

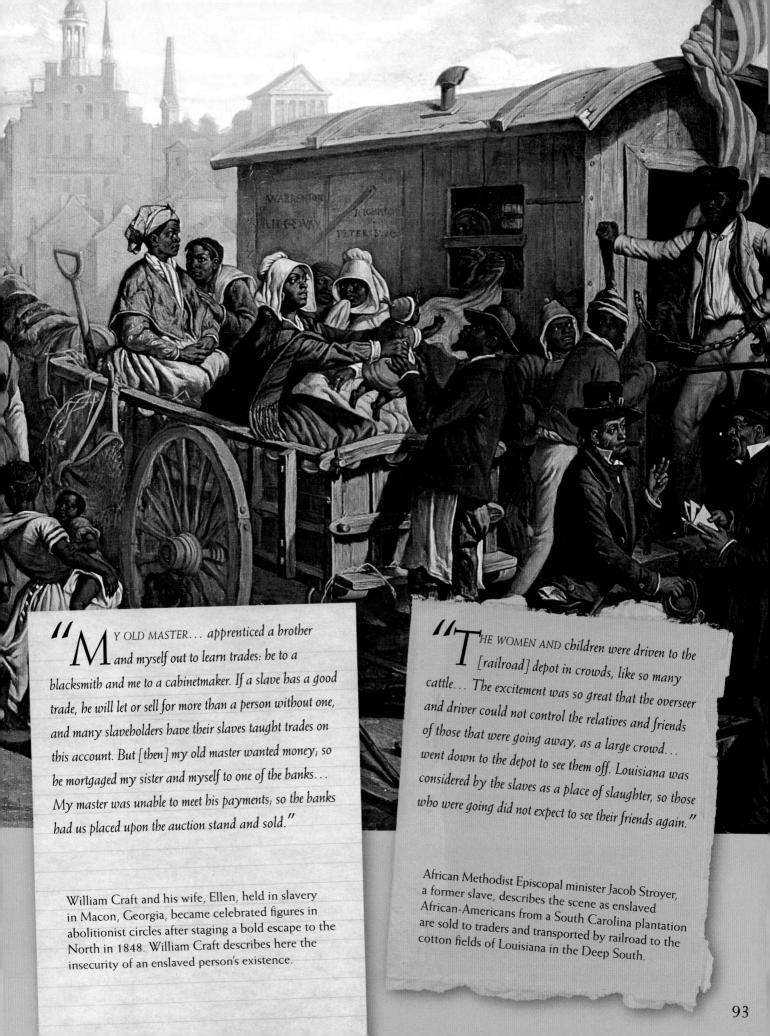

"MY OLD MASTER... apprenticed a brother and myself out to learn trades: he to a blacksmith and me to a cabinetmaker. If a slave has a good trade, he will let or sell for more than a person without one, and many slaveholders have their slaves taught trades on this account. But [then] my old master wanted money; so he mortgaged my sister and myself to one of the banks... My master was unable to meet his payments; so the banks had us placed upon the auction stand and sold."

William Craft and his wife, Ellen, held in slavery in Macon, Georgia, became celebrated figures in abolitionist circles after staging a bold escape to the North in 1848. William Craft describes here the insecurity of an enslaved person's existence.

"THE WOMEN AND children were driven to the [railroad] depot in crowds, like so many cattle... The excitement was so great that the overseer and driver could not control the relatives and friends of those that were going away, as a large crowd... went down to the depot to see them off. Louisiana was considered by the slaves as a place of slaughter, so those who were going did not expect to see their friends again."

African Methodist Episcopal minister Jacob Stroyer, a former slave, describes the scene as enslaved African-Americans from a South Carolina plantation are sold to traders and transported by railroad to the cotton fields of Louisiana in the Deep South.

PLANTATION LIFE

Field slave
At work from first light until sunset, under constant threat of the whip, the enslaved men and women who worked in the fields had the hardest life on the plantation. At harvest time slaves sometimes labored as many as 18 hours a day.

A SLAVE PLANTATION in the Southern United States in the first half of the 19th century was an enclosed world based on brutal oppression. The enslaved adults and children played different roles within this community—roles dictated by the different kinds of work that needed to be done.

Slave drivers
Drivers were trusted slaves who had been promoted to a role as assistants to the white overseer. They whipped fellow slaves when ordered to do so, knowing that if they refused they themselves would be flogged.

House slave

Some enslaved men and women worked around the master's house, cooking, cleaning, looking after children, and serving at table. They were provided with better food and clothing than those in the fields, but they were still at their owner's beck and call and subject to physical punishment at the owner's whim.

Living conditions

The enslaved were housed in overcrowded cabins lacking in basic comforts—in stark contrast to the big house of the plantation owners. They often slept on a bare mud floor, wrapped in blankets. Their homes offered little protection against heat, cold, or damp.

Children together

Up to about the age of eight, children born into slavery on the plantation often had lots of free time. They also mixed freely with white children. As they grew older, the slave children were put to work and carefully separated from their white childhood friends.

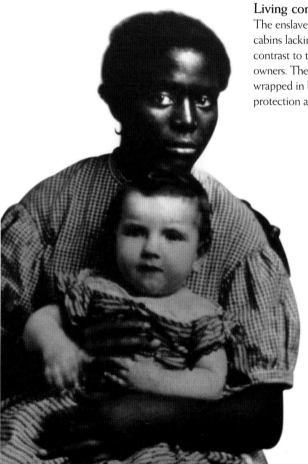

Brought up by slaves

Slave owners entrusted their children to enslaved women for most of their early years. An enslaved woman was often the very first object of childhood affection that a member of a slave-owning family could remember.

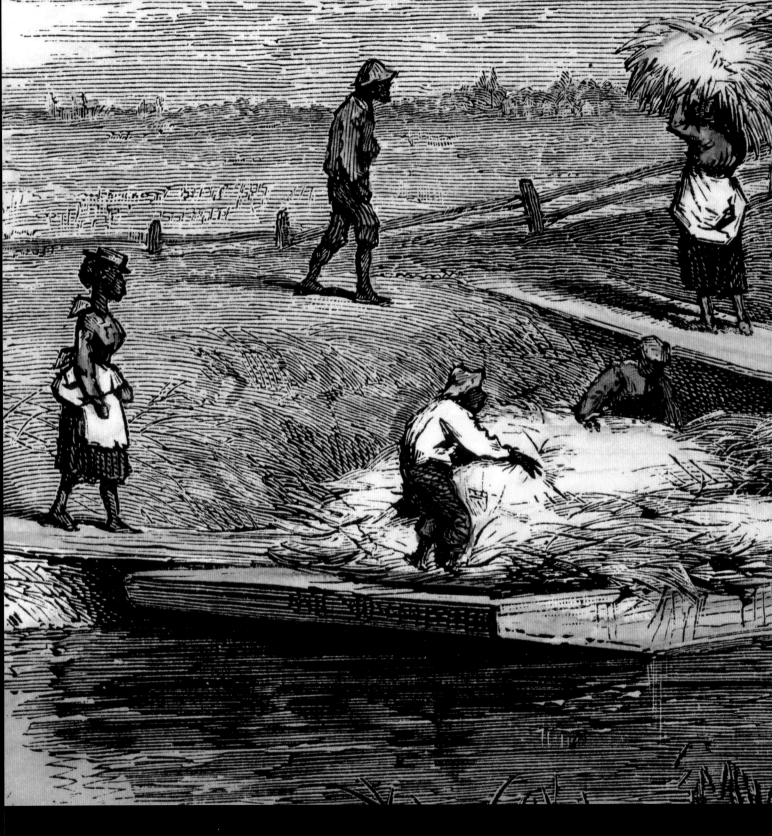

"Every slave have task to do, sometime one task, sometime two, and sometime three. You have for work till task through… If slave don't do task, they get licking with lash on naked back."

Sam Polite, former slave, interviewed about his memories of plantation work, aged 93

ACHIEVEMENT AGAINST THE ODDS

WITH THE ODDS STACKED against them, enslaved people stubbornly and courageously improved their lives. Some developed craft skills and worked as artisans, keeping some of the money they earned for themselves. Others sold crops they grew. A few achieved a literate education, although there were laws against this in the Southern United States. Increasing numbers gained freedom and some rose to prominence through their outstanding talents.

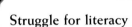

Struggle for literacy
Learning to read and write was the key for an enslaved person to find a link to a wider world. Despite laws banning the teaching of letters to the enslaved, many did achieve literacy, with or without their owner's approval.

Making money
Enslaved women who grew food on a plantation were often allowed to sell any surplus they produced. This gave them an income that they could use to make small improvements in their lives. Some earned enough money through various forms of work or trade to buy freedom for themselves and their family.

Gaining freedom
Thousands of enslaved people were freed over time. An owner might free slaves as a reward for service, or because he no longer needed them. Sometimes slaves were freed because they were the children of an enslaved woman and a white slave owner—the slave owner would free his own kin. Or the enslaved freed themselves by purchase, escape, or revolt.

Successful businessman
Philadelphia-born James Forten was a rare example of a prospering African-American in the age of slavery. Born free but poor, he rose by his own efforts in the late 18th century to be a successful sailmaker with a very substantial fortune.

Despite writing poems that were much admired, Phillis Wheatley died in poverty.

Prominent poet
Born in Gambia, Phillis Wheatley was brought to America as a child on a slave ship. She was taught to read by her owners in Boston. She published her first poetry in 1770 at age 17 and her merit was widely recognized. This statue of Wheatley writing poetry is part of the Boston Women's Memorial.

Man of many talents
Ignatius Sancho was born on a slave ship in the 1720s but grew up to become a well-known figure in London. Dubbed "the extraordinary Negro," he ran a store, wrote music, acted in the theater, and published a book of musical theory. His portrait was painted by the fashionable 18th-century artist Allan Ramsay.

99

FREE PEOPLE OF COLOR

THROUGHOUT THE ERA OF SLAVERY, free people of full or partial African descent were to be found everywhere in the Americas. These free people of color included businessmen, landowners, doctors, craftsmen, and storeowners, as well as many poor folk. Initially, there were fewer free black people in North America than in the Caribbean or Brazil, but their numbers increased rapidly from the late 18th century. Liberated from slavery, they were oppressed by racial prejudice and discrimination.

Putting on style
Free people of color often adopted European manners and dress as a way of asserting their liberty. By doing this, they distanced themselves from their past—and infuriated white racists.

Landowners of color
On some Caribbean islands—for example, Haiti and Trinidad—free people of color were among the largest landowners in the 18th century. Although they used slave labor on their plantations, they were themselves still victims of racism, denied equality with whites.

New Orleans
The Louisiana port of New Orleans was a major center of free colored life. People of color owned much of the property and business in the city by the early 19th century, giving New Orleans its distinctive cultural style and atmosphere.

Black in Britain

Britain acquired a substantial free black population in the course of the 18th century, mostly people who had once been slaves in the Americas. One of the best known was Francis Barber, the servant of the eminent literary figure Dr. Johnson. Johnson left most of his possessions to Barber when he died.

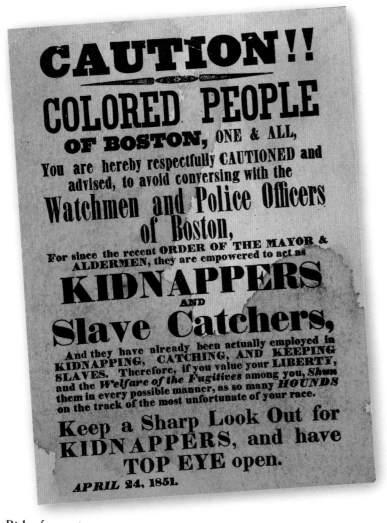

CAUTION!!

COLORED PEOPLE
OF BOSTON, ONE & ALL,
You are hereby respectfully CAUTIONED and advised, to avoid conversing with the
Watchmen and Police Officers
of Boston,
For since the recent ORDER OF THE MAYOR & ALDERMEN, they are empowered to act as
KIDNAPPERS
AND
Slave Catchers,
And they have already been actually employed in KIDNAPPING, CATCHING, AND KEEPING SLAVES. Therefore, if you value your LIBERTY, and the *Welfare of the Fugitives* among you, *Shun* them in every possible manner, as so many *HOUNDS* on the track of the most unfortunate of your race.

Keep a Sharp Look Out for
KIDNAPPERS, and have
TOP EYE open.
APRIL 24, 1851.

Color bar

The more free people of color there were in the United States, the more they tended to be resented, feared, and restricted by white society. In the non-slave states of the North, African-Americans were excluded from places of entertainment and from churches. They were also prevented from sharing public transportation with white passengers. Here, a white man attempts to order a black man off a train.

Risk of recapture

A free person of color was always at risk of being enslaved in the United States. This poster warns Bostonians of the activities of slave-catchers, who would seize free blacks and carry them south into slavery, claiming they were fugitive slaves.

Organizing for freedom

Some free people of color became antiracist campaigners. Absalom Jones was one of the founders of the Free African Society in Philadelphia in 1787. The society helped free individuals and campaigned on political issues.

VOICES BLACK IN THE US

Many African-Americans in the Northern United States had earned or had been granted freedom by the first half of the 19th century. But they were still subjected to many indignities based on their color. They desired simply to be treated as equal human beings, but most white Americans thought black people inferior and did not want to mix with them.

"I REMEMBER ABOUT two years ago there was in Boston, near the southwest corner of Boston Common, a menagerie. I had long desired to see such a collection as I understood was being exhibited there. Never having had an opportunity while a slave, I resolved to seize this, and as I approached the entrance to gain admission, I was told by the door-keeper, in a harsh and contemptuous tone, 'We don't allow niggers in here.' I also remember attending a revival meeting in the Rev. Henry Jackson's meeting-house, at New Bedford, and going up the broad aisle for a seat, I was met by a good deacon, who told me in a pious tone, 'We don't allow niggers in here.'"

The abolitionist Frederick Douglass escaped to freedom in the Northern United States from slavery in the South in 1838, at the age of 20. He found the racism of whites in the North almost as intolerable as the slave owners of the South and detailed many examples of the racial segregation practiced in the Northern states.

"I HAVE MET girls in the schoolroom—they have been thoroughly kind and cordial to me—perhaps the next day met them in the street—they feared to recognize me; these I can but regard now with scorn and contempt... Even to the child's mind they reveal volumes of deceit and heartlessness, and early teach a lesson of suspicion and distrust."

Charlotte Forten was born into a prosperous free black family in Philadelphia in 1837. This diary excerpt records her experience, age 17, as the only non-white pupil at a school in Salem, Massachusetts. Forten became an activist for the abolition of slavery.

"WHEN I FIRST went to the Northern states, which is about ten years ago, although I was free as to the law, I was made to feel severely the difference between persons of different colors. No black man was admitted to the same seats in churches with the whites, nor to the inside of public conveyances, nor into street coaches or cabs: we had to be content with the decks of steamboats in all weathers... in various other ways, we were treated as though we were of a race of men below the whites."

Moses Grandy, a fugitive from slavery in the Southern United States, wrote his autobiography *Life of a Slave* in 1843. Despite his experience of racial segregation as a free person of color in the North, he believed that through the efforts of abolitionists the situation was improving.

AFRICAN-AMERICANS AND CHRISTIANITY

AT FIRST, ENSLAVED PEOPLE held to their own African religions, regarding their masters' religion with suspicion. Slave owners were unwilling to allow their slaves to be converted, fearing they would demand full rights as Christians. But over time enslaved people found strength in the Christian faith. In the United States and the Caribbean, churches founded by free blacks became centers of education and of action for political change.

Against the establishment
Efforts to Christianize the enslaved were spearheaded by sects such as the Methodists and Baptists, who often preached at open-air meetings, above. Churches were usually segregated, with African-Americans having their own gallery.

Christian obedience
By the 1800s, many slave owners were providing their slaves with some form of Christian instruction and rites, although they stressed the elements of Christianity that taught obedience. Some slave owners even invited black ministers to preach to their slaves, as on this plantation in South Carolina.

West Indian slave owners regarded Methodists who preached to the enslaved as dangerous subversives.

Moses and liberation
The enslaved responded to the liberating message of parts of the Bible. The story of Moses leading his people to freedom inspired African-Americans wishing to escape bondage.

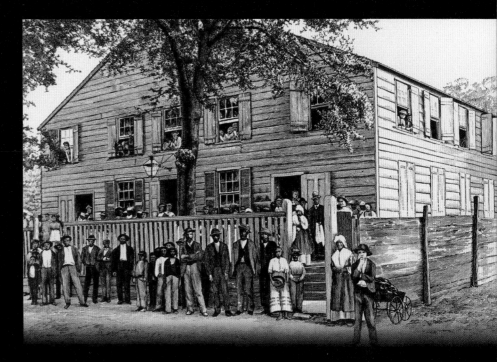

Black Baptist church
White Methodists and Baptists had mixed views on slavery and race, leading believers of African descent to form their own churches. The First African Baptist Church was founded by George Liele in Georgia in 1777. He later went to Jamaica, where Baptists won many converts among people of African descent.

African Methodist Episcopal Church
Richard Allen, a free person of color, founded the AME church in 1794 after black Methodists in Philadelphia met restrictions and racist insults from white Methodists.

Distinctive faith
African-Americans made Christianity their own, developing variations on the faith. In the Southern United States, black Baptists practiced an ecstatic religion that had a place for spirit possession and rebirth. This person is being baptized in a Texas river.

Trickster tales
Told and retold among the enslaved, traditional African stories evolved into tales that became familiar to all Americans. Many feature mischievous animal tricksters such as Br'er Rabbit who, like many of the enslaved, survived through cunning to outsmart powerful opponents.

BUILDING A CULTURE

WHEN AFRICANS WERE BROUGHT to the Americas they had no common culture or language. They developed an identity through the bitter experience of enslavement. Based on varied African and European influences, this culture was transmitted from generation to generation by word of mouth. In music, it laid the foundations of jazz, blues, rock and roll, and pop music.

Voodoo ceremonies
The enslaved developed religious practices that combined West African and Christian elements, such as Santeria in Cuba and Voodoo in Haiti and Louisiana. Voodoo rituals and magic helped the spiritual survival of the uprooted.

Capoeira
In Brazil, enslaved people from Africa created capoeira, a spectacular cross between combat training and ritual dance. Similar to Asian martial arts, capoeira was probably based on African war dances. Some believe that it was a disguised way of preparing people to fight in a slave revolt.

African drumming
Drums and rhythm were at the heart of African music and became central to African-American music, too. In South Carolina and Georgia, laws were passed banning slaves from beating drums, as they might be used to signal an uprising.

Slave song
The enslaved expressed themselves in religious songs (known as spirituals) and work songs with distinctive rhythms and harmonies. The famous abolitionist Frederick Douglass wrote that "The songs of the slave represent the sorrows of his heart." But the enslaved also sang songs that expressed the entire range of human emotions, including joy and happiness.

Musical instruments
The enslaved adapted African instruments and adopted European ones. They invented the banjo, evolved from forms of lute traditionally played by "griots"— West African musicians and storytellers.

Lively dance
Exuberant dance was at the heart of African-American self-expression in all forms of celebration and ceremony. Workshops are run to teach African-American children about their cultural and musical heritage—traditional dancing to African drums can still be seen in New Orleans today.

THE FIGHT FOR FREEDOM

THE SECOND HALF of the 18th century was a time of revolutionary upheaval. Slavery was questioned by whites who believed that all people should be free. Both these whites and blacks, who had resisted oppression for years, campaigned for abolition. By the early 19th century, the outlawing of the slave trade was in progress, although it did not finally end for years.

Voting to abolish slavery in France
In February 1794, during the French Revolution, the new revolutionary government in Paris voted to abolished slavery. When Emperor Napoleon came to power a few years later, he overturned their vote and restored it. France finally abolished slavery in 1848.

In Massachusetts, a court case in effect outlaws slavery in the state

Former slave Olaudah Equiano publishes his life story

New York adopts a law for the gradual emancipation of slaves

Lord Dunmore, British governor of Virginia, promises slaves freedom if they fight American rebels

An anti-slave trade society begins a major campaign in Britain

Zachary Macaulay is governor of Sierra Leone, where the British settle freed slaves

Denmark is the first country to ban the slave trade

| 1772 | 1775 | 1776 | 1783 | 1784 | 1787 | 1789 | 1793 | 1794 | 1799 | 1802 | 1804 |

The Somerset case establishes that slavery is illegal on British soil

The US Declaration of Independence states that all men have a right to liberty

The US Constitution allows slavery to continue

The French revolutionary government outlaws slavery in its colonies; it is restored in 1802

New Jersey is the last Northern state in the US to adopt an emancipation law

The Pennsylvania Abolition Society is founded to campaign against slavery

French revolutionaries adopt a Declaration of the Rights of Man

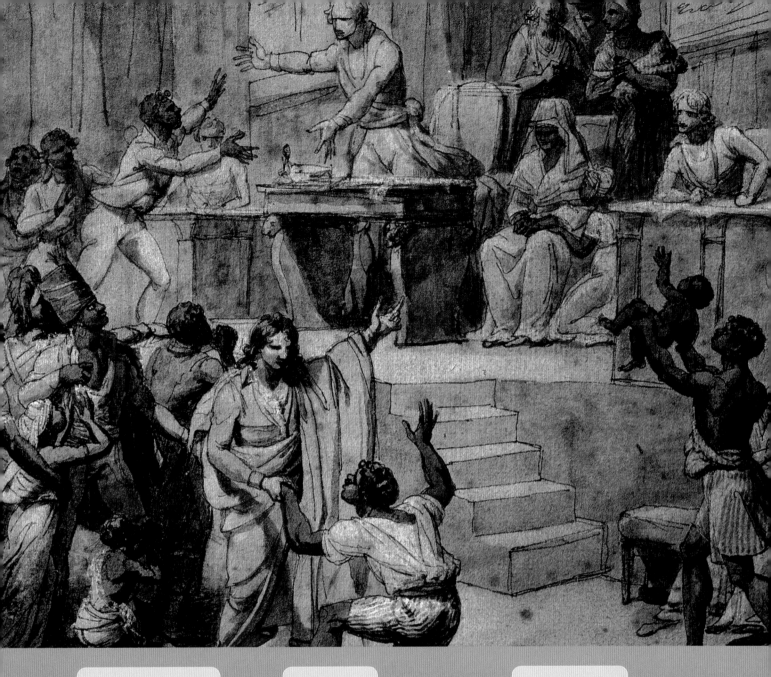

At the Congress of Vienna, the major European powers in principle denounce the slave trade

British ships stationed off West Africa to intercept slave traders

Enslaved Africans on the slave ship *Amistad* seize control of the ship

Britain declares the abolition of the slave trade

Spain agrees to end slave trading north of the equator

The first African-Americans are sent to Liberia by the American Colonization Society

The US declares the enslaved Africans from the *Amistad* free to return to Africa

| 1807 | 1808 | 1814–15 | 1816 | 1817 | 1819 | 1820 | 1822 | 1836 | 1839 | 1841 | 1847 |

The US ends slave trading

The American Colonization Society is founded to return former slaves to Africa

Spain agrees to end all slave trading to the Americas, but large-scale slave imports into Cuba continue

Liberia is declared an independent republic

Portugal officially agrees to abolish the slave trade

QUESTIONING SLAVERY

IN THE 18TH CENTURY, new political and religious ideas in Europe and North America brought slavery into question. Increasing numbers of Christians, inspired by their religious beliefs and a desire for moral improvement, questioned the traditional acceptance of slavery by established churches. At the same time, the movement known as "The Enlightenment" proposed that all men were born equal and had a natural right to freedom. From these revolutionary ideas and beliefs, black people saw a chance of freedom, demanding for themselves the rights that white people had.

Wesley against slavery
John Wesley, the founder of the Methodist movement, was an inspired preacher, famous for his open-air meetings. He led a religious revival in 18th-century Britain. Wesley thought that slavery offended Christian belief.

Quaker meeting
The Quakers, or Society of Friends, is a Christian movement that encourages its members to search their own consciences. Quakers were among the first opponents of slavery in North America, although the Society was deeply divided on the issue for many years.

Quakers were morally against the idea of slavery, yet many still owned slaves themselves.

Unclear awakening
Even Christians who embraced new religious ideas were far from united on slavery. George Whitefield was a leading preacher in the religious revival called "The Great Awakening" in North America in the 1740s. Yet Whitefield used slaves at the Bethesda orphanage he

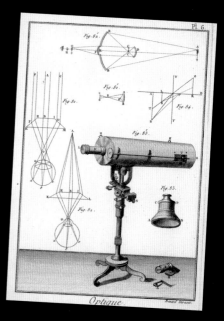

Age of Enlightenment

A belief in science, reason, and human progress developed among the 18th-century educated elite. Men such as Voltaire in France and the American Benjamin Franklin asserted freedom of thought and the natural rights of the individual, and proposed humane and tolerant laws. This illustration is from a famous encyclopedia put together by French Enlightenment thinkers, whose goal was to share knowledge with everyone.

Revolutionary principles

The assertion of individual freedom and rights led to a revolution in America in the 1770s, and in France in 1789. These were accompanied by declarations of principle such as the United States Bill of Rights. Here, the French plant a "liberty tree" to symbolize their new beliefs.

Free enterprise

New economic ideas reinforced opposition to slavery. In his 1776 book *The Wealth of Nations*, Scottish economist and philosopher Adam Smith argued that slavery should be replaced by wage labor.

Crispus Attucks
In March 1770, British troops fired on a crowd in Boston, Massachusetts, killing five people. One of them was a free African-American, Crispus Attucks. Since this Boston Massacre was one of the events that triggered mounting opposition to British rule, Attucks is sometimes seen as the first martyr of the Revolutionary War.

INDEPENDENCE FOR ALL?

THE UNITED STATES WAS FOUNDED in 1776 after colonists in North America rebelled against British rule. They proclaimed independence in the name of freedom, and against "slavery" imposed on them by Britain. Yet in this new country based on principles of liberty and equality, enslaved African-Americans made up one-in-five of the population. Many of those who signed the Declaration of Independence were slave owners. African-Americans fought on both sides in the Revolutionary War, choosing whichever side offered the best hope of freedom. The conflict over slavery would eventually lead to civil war.

Declaration of Independence
The United States was founded by the signing of the Declaration of Independence on July 4, 1776. It stated that all men had the right to "life and liberty, and the pursuit of happiness," but excluded any commitment to the abolition of slavery. A majority of the 56 signatories (known as the Founding Fathers) owned slaves.

Tom Paine
English radical Tom Paine was an enthusiastic supporter of the Revolutionary War. He called for full rights to be extended to slaves, pointing out the hypocrisy of calling British rule "slavery" while keeping a black population enslaved. Only a minority of the American rebels agreed with him.

Thomas Jefferson
The Declaration of Independence's main author was Thomas Jefferson, pictured above on an election banner. Although a slave owner, he thought that slavery was bad for America and blamed the British. However, he believed that abolition was not possible, viewing African-Americans as fundamentally inferior to white Americans.

Revolutionary soldiers
Substantial numbers of African-Americans fought for US independence. Former slave Salem Poor was one of the heroes who fought on the American side at the Battle of Bunker Hill in June 1775.

Dunmore's soldiers
Lord Dunmore, British governor of Virginia, promised freedom to any slave who would bear arms against the rebels. He formed a force of troops known as the Ethiopian Regiment (seen here in a modern-day reenactment at the Colonial Williamsburg Foundation). These troops were among the first of many African-Americans to fight on the British side.

About 100,000 people escaped slavery during the Revolutionary War.

Washington's attitude
Rebel commander George Washington refused to recruit African-Americans, but a shortage of soldiers changed his mind. Several made the winter crossing of the Delaware River with him in 1776—one of the recruits is portrayed here in the bow of the boat.

Agreeing on a constitution
In 1787, a Constitutional Convention thrashed out an agreement between different states on how the United States was to be governed. The Southern states ensured that the new Constitution did not extend freedom to the enslaved. The slave trade was allowed to continue for another two decades. But in the same year, the states also agreed to exclude slavery from the Northwest Territory—the future states of Ohio, Illinois, Indiana, Michigan, and Wisconsin.

THE UNITED STATES DIVIDED

AFTER INDEPENDENCE the Northern states of the United States moved down the path toward freeing their slaves—some states quickly, others more slowly. But the Southern states insisted on preserving slavery, which they saw as fundamental to their economy and society. In fact, the number of enslaved people in the Southern states grew rapidly in the decades after independence, and continued to rise even after a ban on the import of slaves came into effect in 1808.

By 1790, almost 95 percent of US slaves lived in the Southern states.

Emancipation in the Northern states
The states with fewest slaves freed them quickest. Vermont, which had almost none, took the lead. In Massachusetts and New Hampshire, courts outlawed slavery in 1783. Other Northern states adopted gradual emancipation. Typically, this offered freedom to anyone born after a certain date, often with the condition that they continued to act as servants until adulthood. New York made a definite end to slavery in 1827. In other states, there were still a few slaves in the 1840s.

STATE	EUROPEAN SETTLEMENT	SLAVERY FIRST RECORDED	SLAVERY ABOLISHED
Massachusetts	1620	1629	1783
New Hampshire	1623	1645	1783
New Jersey	1620	1626	1804–46
New York	1624	1626	1799–1827
Connecticut	1633	1639	1784–1840s
Rhode Island	1636	1652	1784–1842
Pennsylvania	1638	1639	1780–1840s
Vermont	1666	1760	1777

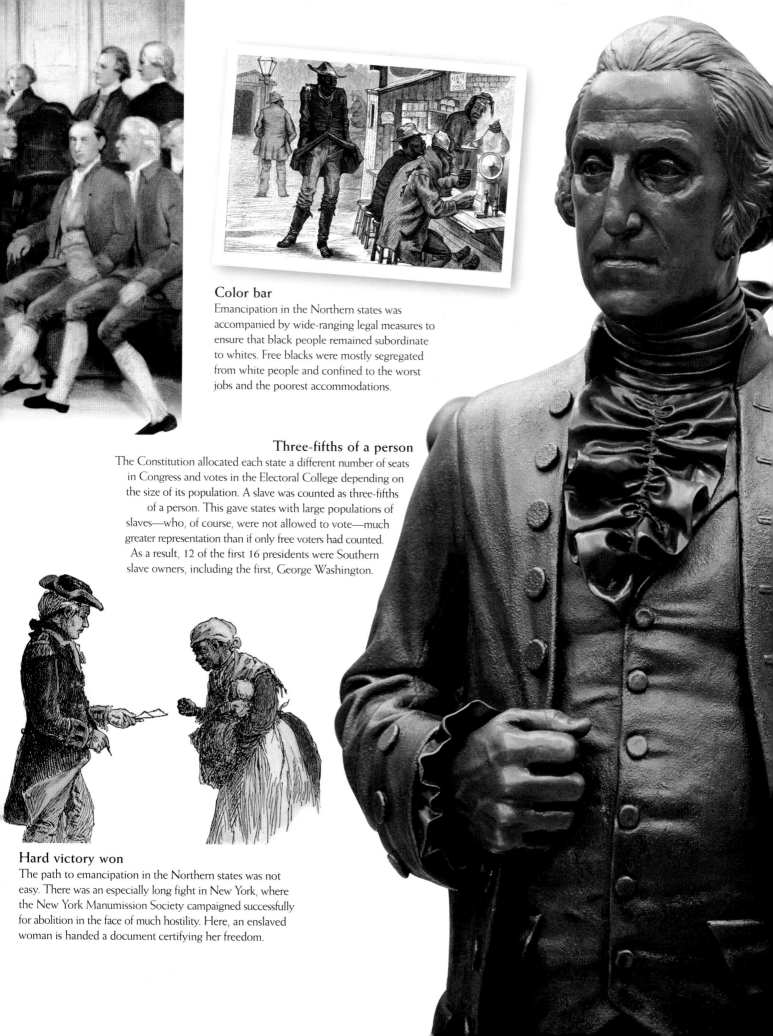

Color bar

Emancipation in the Northern states was accompanied by wide-ranging legal measures to ensure that black people remained subordinate to whites. Free blacks were mostly segregated from white people and confined to the worst jobs and the poorest accommodations.

Three-fifths of a person

The Constitution allocated each state a different number of seats in Congress and votes in the Electoral College depending on the size of its population. A slave was counted as three-fifths of a person. This gave states with large populations of slaves—who, of course, were not allowed to vote—much greater representation than if only free voters had counted. As a result, 12 of the first 16 presidents were Southern slave owners, including the first, George Washington.

Hard victory won

The path to emancipation in the Northern states was not easy. There was an especially long fight in New York, where the New York Manumission Society campaigned successfully for abolition in the face of much hostility. Here, an enslaved woman is handed a document certifying her freedom.

VOICES
AMERICAN
EFFORTS

Many of the liberal-minded gentlemen who led the revolution that created the United States of America in 1776 were in principle strongly opposed to slavery, even if they were slave owners themselves. But their commitment to any practical plan for the abolition of slavery was limited in most cases by self-interest and by a racist belief in the inferiority of black people, whom they could not accept as equal citizens.

"Is IT NOT amazing that… in a country above all others fond of liberty, that in such an age, and such a country we find men, professing a religion the most humane, mild, meek, gentle, and generous; adopting a principle [slavery] as repugnant to humanity as it is inconsistent with the Bible and destructive to liberty… Would any one believe that I am master of slaves of my own purchase! I am drawn along by the general inconvenience of living without them, I will not, I cannot justify it… I believe a time will come when an opportunity will be offered to abolish this lamentable evil. Everything we can do is to improve it, if it happens in our day, if not, let us transmit to our descendants together with our slaves, a pity for their unhappy lot, and an abhorrence for slavery."

Patrick Henry, a lawyer from Virginia, was a prominent figure in the Revolutionary War, especially famous for his cry, "Give me liberty, or give me death!" This quote is from a letter he wrote to his friend Robert Pleasants in January 1773.

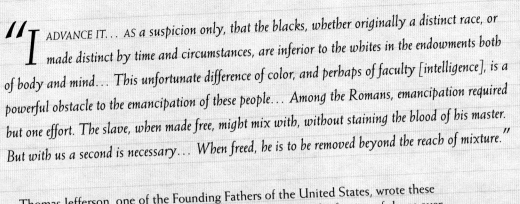

"I ADVANCE IT... AS a suspicion only, that the blacks, whether originally a distinct race, or made distinct by time and circumstances, are inferior to the whites in the endowments both of body and mind... This unfortunate difference of color, and perhaps of faculty [intelligence], is a powerful obstacle to the emancipation of these people... Among the Romans, emancipation required but one effort. The slave, when made free, might mix with, without staining the blood of his master. But with us a second is necessary... When freed, he is to be removed beyond the reach of mixture."

Thomas Jefferson, one of the Founding Fathers of the United States, wrote these words in 1781. Jefferson favored gradual emancipation—the freeing of slaves over a period of time—but he believed that freed slaves should be returned to Africa.

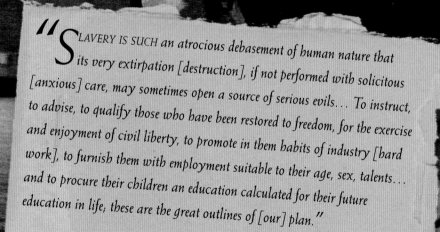

"SLAVERY IS SUCH an atrocious debasement of human nature that its very extirpation [destruction], if not performed with solicitous [anxious] care, may sometimes open a source of serious evils... To instruct, to advise, to qualify those who have been restored to freedom, for the exercise and enjoyment of civil liberty, to promote in them habits of industry [hard work], to furnish them with employment suitable to their age, sex, talents... and to procure their children an education calculated for their future education in life; these are the great outlines of [our] plan."

Benjamin Franklin was another Founding Father of the United States. Although he did own slaves in his younger years, Franklin became a whole-hearted opponent of slavery. He wrote these words in 1789 as president of the Philadelphia Abolition Society.

Olaudah Equiano
Although most black people in Britain were poor, some were educated and came to mix in privileged circles. One of them was Olaudah Equiano, who became a leading anti-slavery campaigner in London. His story of his life as a slave, published in 1789, had a powerful impact on public opinion.

CAMPAIGNERS IN BRITAIN

AS THE MAIN SLAVE-TRADING NATION, with the world's largest empire in which slaves were widely exploited, Britain's attitude to slavery was crucial. From the 1770s, a number of people in Britain began to work for its abolition, including the philanthropist Granville Sharp and former slaves such as Olaudah Equiano. They started by challenging the legality of slavery on British soil, achieving landmark decisions in key court cases.

Olaudah Equiano's autobiography was a best-seller of its time—nine editions and several translations were made in his lifetime.

Life in Britain
In the late 1700s, there were thousands of black people in Britain. Some were slaves who had traveled with their owners. Some were free blacks who had come to Britain after working on ships or after joining the British side in the Revolutionary War. A few, such as the composer and violinist Joseph Emidy, became celebrated public figures.

Granville Sharp and Jonathan Strong

An important figure in the anti-slavery campaign was the Englishman Granville Sharp. He first became involved in the fate of slaves in Britain through the case of Jonathan Strong, a mistreated slave whom Sharp rescued from his owner in London. Here, Sharp restrains a sea captain from taking Strong for shipment to Jamaica, after winning the case for his release.

The Somerset case

Sharp also took up the case of James Somerset, a slave who escaped from his London owner, but was captured and put on a ship for Jamaica. Sharp arranged for a writ demanding that he be freed. The court's decision in Somerset's favor in 1772 spelled the end of slave ownership on British soil.

Mansfield's judgment

The Somerset case was tried by Lord Chief Justice Mansfield. He ruled that slavery was totally unacceptable and could only exist if established by law. But in Britain no such law had been passed. Mansfield did not intend to declare slavery illegal, but in effect he did.

In 1781, the captain of a British slave ship, the Zong, threw 133 Africans overboard in the mid-Atlantic. The owners of the human cargo claimed insurance money for the loss and took the insurers to court when they refused to pay. The case became a rallying cry for the British abolitionist movement, thanks to the efforts of Equiano and another abolitionist, Thomas Clarkson.

ABOLISHING THE SLAVE TRADE

Thomas Clarkson
As a student at Cambridge University, destined for a career in the church, Clarkson wrote an essay denouncing slavery. This led him to devote his life to the anti-slavery cause. From 1787, he worked tirelessly to accumulate and publicize information on the evils of the slave trade.

IN 1787, ANTI-SLAVERY ACTIVISTS in Britain formed the Society for Effecting the Abolition of the Slave Trade. The society mounted a mass campaign to pressure the British parliament into banning the slave trade—chosen as an easier objective than the abolition of slavery itself. Britain was not a democracy, and opposition to abolition of the trade was strong in parliament, where slave traders and West Indian plantation owners were heavily represented. British ships were finally banned from carrying slaves in 1807.

William Wilberforce
A pious conservative in most of his political views, William Wilberforce led the anti-slave trade cause in the British parliament. With his strong moral conscience and passionate speeches, Wilberforce was the ideal person to champion the movement in parliament— where those who were undecided needed to be converted to the abolitionist cause.

Medallion
Thomas Wedgwood, a pottery manufacturer, supported the anti-slave trade campaign. As part of the propaganda for the movement, he mass-produced a medallion with the motto "Am I Not a Man and a Brother." Showing a slave in chains, gratefully and piously awaiting freedom, it was created to appeal to white sentiment.

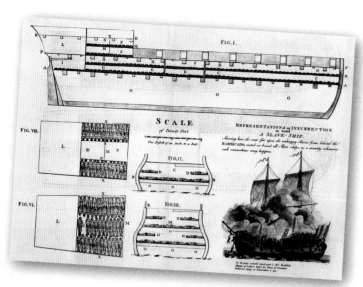

Mass anti-slavery campaign
The anti-slave trade campaign has been described as the world's first modern mass political campaign. A consumer boycott of slave-produced sugar was organized, petitions were signed, and large public meetings held. The campaign won massive support from the British people.

Tightly packed slave ship
The document above shows how Africans were kept on board the slave ship *Brookes*—with very little room to move, conditions were appalling. Produced in 1788, it became the movement's most effective propaganda image.

The British campaign against the slave trade took 20 years to succeed.

Debate in parliament
The goal of the anti-slavery campaign was to pressure parliament into passing a law banning the slave trade. A parliamentary inquiry uncovered the horrors of the slave trade, with testimony from many slave captains, but a series of votes in parliament failed to produce an anti-slave trade majority.

Celebrating abolition
In 1807, the British parliament voted on the abolition of the slave trade for the twelfth time. This occasion, they agreed, by a large majority, to the ban. Abolition enabled the British to present themselves as champions of freedom, although the rest of the world remembered how long Britain had taken the lead in the slave trade.

VOICES
BRITISH ABOLITIONISTS

The leaders of the British campaign for abolition of the slave trade were mostly devout Christians who had a powerful sense of guilt about the suffering and injustice their country was causing. These campaigners were assisted by freed African slaves such as Olaudah Equiano and Ottobah Cugoano, who made important contributions to the anti-slave trade movement.

"I MEAN NOT to accuse anyone, but to take the shame upon myself, in common, indeed, with the whole parliament of Great Britain, for having suffered this horrid trade to be carried on under their authority. We are all guilty—we ought all to plead guilty... As soon as ever I had arrived thus far in my investigation of the slave trade, I confess to you, sir, so enormous, so dreadful, so irremediable did its wickedness appear that my own mind was completely made up for the abolition."

William Wilberforce made this speech to the British parliament in May 1789, proposing the first bill for the abolition of the slave trade. Wilberforce also worked for a stricter observance of Sunday as a holy day and closely with the Royal Society for the Prevention of Cruelty to Animals.

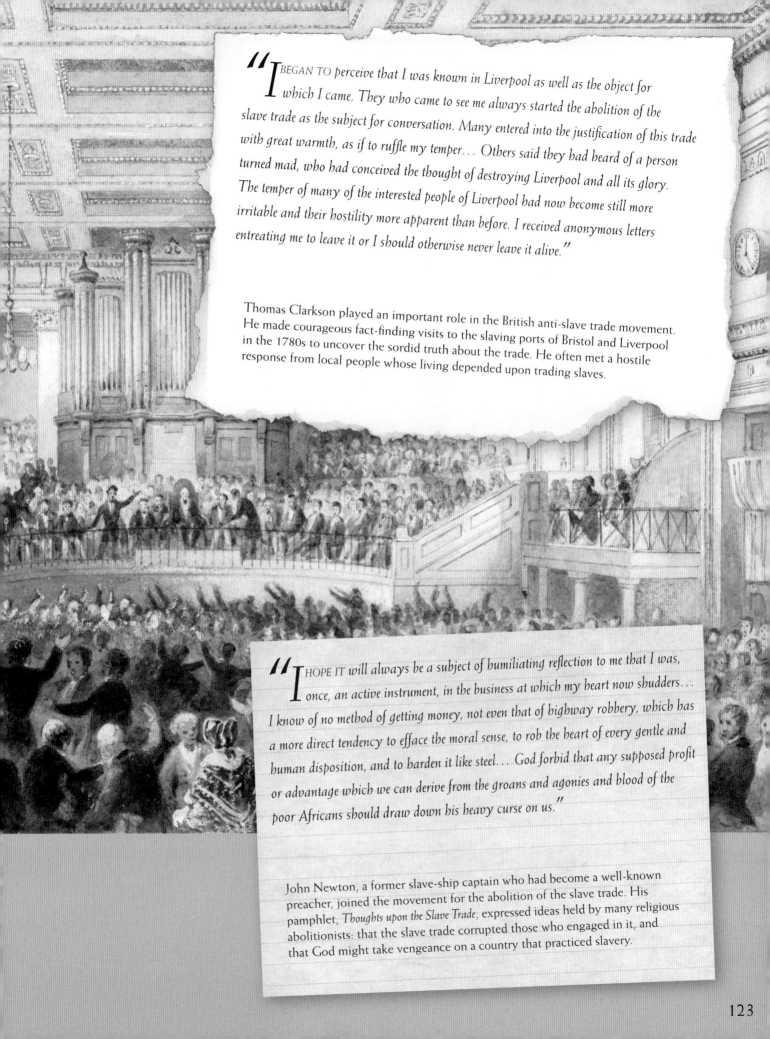

"I BEGAN TO perceive that I was known in Liverpool as well as the object for which I came. They who came to see me always started the abolition of the slave trade as the subject for conversation. Many entered into the justification of this trade with great warmth, as if to ruffle my temper... Others said they had heard of a person turned mad, who had conceived the thought of destroying Liverpool and all its glory. The temper of many of the interested people of Liverpool had now become still more irritable and their hostility more apparent than before. I received anonymous letters entreating me to leave it or I should otherwise never leave it alive."

Thomas Clarkson played an important role in the British anti-slave trade movement. He made courageous fact-finding visits to the slaving ports of Bristol and Liverpool in the 1780s to uncover the sordid truth about the trade. He often met a hostile response from local people whose living depended upon trading slaves.

"I HOPE IT will always be a subject of humiliating reflection to me that I was, once, an active instrument, in the business at which my heart now shudders... I know of no method of getting money, not even that of highway robbery, which has a more direct tendency to efface the moral sense, to rob the heart of every gentle and human disposition, and to harden it like steel... God forbid that any supposed profit or advantage which we can derive from the groans and agonies and blood of the poor Africans should draw down his heavy curse on us."

John Newton, a former slave-ship captain who had become a well-known preacher, joined the movement for the abolition of the slave trade. His pamphlet, *Thoughts upon the Slave Trade*, expressed ideas held by many religious abolitionists: that the slave trade corrupted those who engaged in it, and that God might take vengeance on a country that practiced slavery.

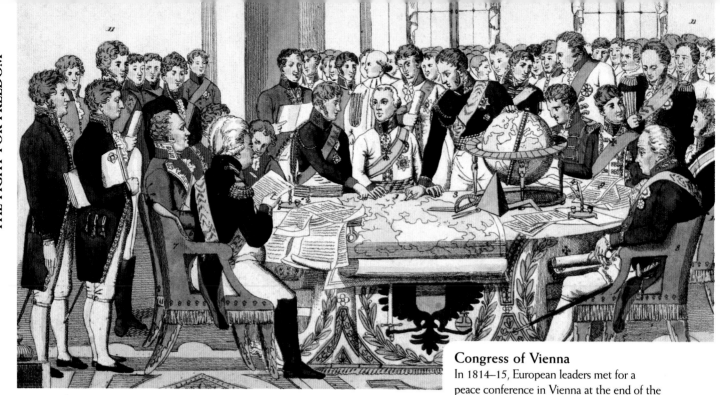

ENFORCING THE BAN

Congress of Vienna
In 1814–15, European leaders met for a peace conference in Vienna at the end of the Napoleonic Wars. Britain, the dominant world power, persuaded other states to make a declaration against the slave trade. It then negotiated agreements with individual states to end slave trading.

THE UNITED STATES CONGRESS enacted a ban on the transatlantic slave trade at virtually the same time as the British parliament. But the Americans made little effort to enforce the ban. Britain, in contrast, launched a sustained campaign to suppress the trade, sending ships to the African coast and negotiating anti-slave trade treaties with other European powers. Such efforts impeded the transatlantic traffic, but they did not end it—about a quarter of all Africans transported across the Atlantic were trafficked after 1807, most of them to Brazil and Cuba.

Banning the slave trade
Denmark was the first country to officially ban the slave trade, with Britain and the United States close behind. Spain, Portugal, and Portugal's former colony Brazil were the main slave-trading nations in the 19th century, making no effort to stop the trade even after agreeing to do so.

COUNTRY	SLAVERY BAN
Denmark	1802
Britain	1807
United States	1808
France	1818
Spain	1820
Portugal	1836
Brazil	1851

West Africa Squadron

Britain established a permanent naval presence off the African coast, the West Africa Squadron, to stop and search suspected slavers. Between 1808 and 1860 about 150,000 African captives were freed by Royal Navy patrols. However, thousands of British sailors lost their lives due to the high risk of disease.

THE AMISTAD

In 1839, enslaved Africans being moved around the Cuban coast seized control of their slave ship, the *Amistad*, killing its captain. The rebels tried to sail the ship to Africa but ended up in Connecticut, and became the object of a legal and political battle. The Spanish demanded their return to Cuba, then a Spanish colony, but former US president John Quincy Adams successfully argued that the Africans had originally been brought to Cuba illegally, in defianse of the slave-trade ban, and they were freed.

Fighting patrol

The Royal Navy's anti-slavery patrols were often defied by slave ships that were fast and well-armed. In 1829, the patrol ship HMS *Black Joke* pursued the Spanish slave ship *El Almirante* off West Africa. After a bitter battle, the patrol ship freed more than 400 slaves on board the Spanish ship.

Cuba imported some 600,000 slaves after the slave trade ban was imposed.

Cuban trade expands

In the 19th century the slave trade to Cuba expanded rapidly. Enslaved Africans were shipped in to work on sugar plantations. The outlawing of the trade was ignored by the Cuban authorities, and slave ships easily evaded anti-slavery patrols. Cuban ports such as Havana were packed with ships exporting slave-produced sugar—much of it bought by countries such as Britain that opposed the trade.

BACK TO AFRICA

FROM THE LATE 1780S ONWARD, there were growing numbers of freed slaves in the United States and Britain. Since integrating these free people of African origin in white-dominated societies was seen by whites as a problem, projects were devised for returning them to Africa. The British tried to settle black people in Sierra Leone, while the Americans used Liberia as a base for African-Americans. The projects were, for the most part, financially and practically unsuccessful for both the sponsors and would-be African settlers.

Zachary Macaulay
The survival of the Sierra Leone settlement was partly due to the efforts of its first governor, the idealistic Zachary Macaulay, who held the job from 1793 to 1799. Later, in the 1820s, Macaulay was a founder of the Anti-Slavery Society.

Sierra Leone Company
The Sierra Leone Company was set up by British anti-slavery campaigners in 1787. The first colonists were drawn from the impoverished black populations of London and other British cities. These settlers were later joined by others from Nova Scotia, Canada, and Jamaica. Many of these settlers were "loyalists," who had supported the British cause during the Revolutionary War.

Freetown
The black people who went to Sierra Leone faced many kinds of hardship and oppression. Despite this, they succeeded in building up a settlement at Freetown on the West African coast. Sierra Leone became a British colony and a place to settle captives who were freed by anti-slave trade patrols.

American Colonization Society
In the 1820s, the American Colonization Society began assisting thousands of black Americans to move to Liberia, in West Africa. Dominated by white people, the society held the view that the presence of a large free black population was bad for the United States. Free people of color saw this as a pro-slavery plot to deport free blacks.

By 1867, the American Colonization Society had moved 13,000 African-Americans to Liberia.

Paul Cuffee
Of mixed African-American and Native-American parentage, Paul Cuffee, seen here in a silhouette engraving, was a ship's captain and successful businessman from Massachusetts. He devised an ambitious plan to settle free African-Americans in Sierra Leone, already populated with those settled by the British. His death in 1817 ended these plans, but Cuffee's example inspired the back-to-Africa movement in the United States.

Hard struggle
There were initially heavy losses among settlers and missionaries in Liberia. Many died from diseases like malaria and yellow fever, others in conflicts with local Africans. Yet the colony lived on, and in 1847 it became the world's first independent black republic.

ABOLISHING SLAVERY IN THE AMERICAS

ABOLISHING SLAVERY was much harder than banning the slave trade. Slave labor was the cornerstone of the economy of the Americas, and was central to the world economy at the time. But the enslaved and free blacks kept up pressure for freedom, while white abolitionists campaigned tirelessly for reform. The British Empire abolished slavery in 1834, and the French in 1848. But in the United States, the struggle took its most dramatic form, with abolition only occurring as a result of civil war.

"Let us bind up the nation's wounds"
Only a month after speaking these hopeful words in his second inaugural address, Lincoln was assassinated. He did not live to see the end of the Civil War or to help reconstruct the war-torn nation.

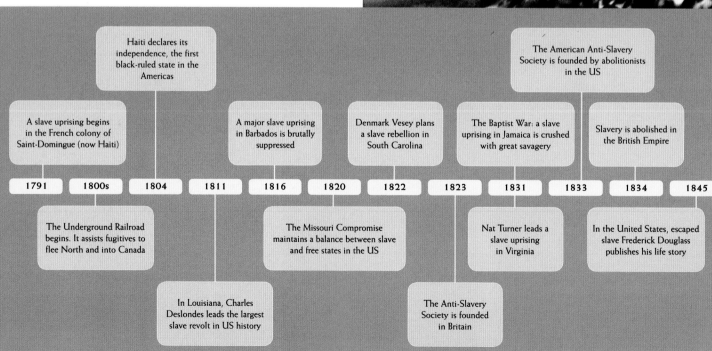

Haiti declares its independence, the first black-ruled state in the Americas

The American Anti-Slavery Society is founded by abolitionists in the US

A slave uprising begins in the French colony of Saint-Domingue (now Haiti)

A major slave uprising in Barbados is brutally suppressed

Denmark Vesey plans a slave rebellion in South Carolina

The Baptist War: a slave uprising in Jamaica is crushed with great savagery

Slavery is abolished in the British Empire

| 1791 | 1800s | 1804 | 1811 | 1816 | 1820 | 1822 | 1823 | 1831 | 1833 | 1834 | 1845 |

The Underground Railroad begins. It assists fugitives to flee North and into Canada

The Missouri Compromise maintains a balance between slave and free states in the US

Nat Turner leads a slave uprising in Virginia

In the United States, escaped slave Frederick Douglass publishes his life story

In Louisiana, Charles Deslondes leads the largest slave revolt in US history

The Anti-Slavery Society is founded in Britain

The Fugitive Slave Act puts all black Americans in the North, whether fugitive slaves or free persons, at risk of kidnapping and enslavement

Republican candidate Abraham Lincoln wins the US presidential election

Thousands of African-Americans enlist in the Union armed forces

Slavery is abolished in Brazil

Slavery is abolished in the French Empire

The Kansas-Nebraska Act leads to fighting between pro- and anti-slavery groups in Kansas

Civil War begins in the US after Southern states leave the Union

After leading the North to victory in the Civil War, Lincoln is assassinated

| 1848 | 1849 | 1850 | 1852 | 1854 | 1859 | 1860 | 1861 | 1863 | 1865 | 1870 | 1888 |

Harriet Tubman escapes from slavery in the southern US

Abolitionist John Brown is executed after leading a raid on Harpers Ferry, Virginia

The Emancipation Proclamation declares slaves free in the rebel states

Spain decrees the gradual emancipation of slaves in its colonies

Harriet Beecher Stowe's anti-slavery novel *Uncle Tom's Cabin* is published

The 13th Amendment to the Constitution abolishes slavery in the US

REBELLION IN HAITI

THE FRENCH-RULED CARIBBEAN COLONY HAITI, then known as Saint-Domingue, was a rich source of slave-produced sugar and coffee. In 1791, as a result of upheaval in France, the colony fell into disorder, and slaves seized the opportunity to rebel. They found an inspired leader in a free black, Toussaint Louverture, who emerged as ruler of the colony after a series of military struggles. Toussaint was later captured and died in prison, but the colonists resisted Emperor Napoleon's attempts to reimpose slavery and founded the first black-ruled state in the New World.

Revolutionary change
In 1789, a revolution broke out in France. The French revolutionaries (seen storming the Bastille prison in Paris, above) granted free blacks a share in running Saint-Domingue with white planters. But the whites refused to comply and executed the free black leaders.

Confused conflict
The slave uprising in Saint-Domingue in 1791 led to the massacre of many hundreds of slave owners. Thousands of slaves were killed in the uprising's suppression, and Saint-Domingue descended into chaos. French, British, and Spanish troops, all at different times, fought with and against black rebels in the colony. Here, French soldiers battle the rebels.

Toussaint Louverture

Although born a slave, Toussaint was a prosperous free black. He took over leadership of the slave revolt through his ability to organize a guerrilla war. A man of great intelligence and dignity, Toussaint tried to found a government based on the principle of racial equality.

France defeated

The French emperor Napoleon Bonaparte, who took power in France in 1799, sent a large army across the sea to reimpose slavery in Saint-Domingue. The rebels defeated Napoleon's army, but Toussaint was taken captive and carried off to a prison in France. He died there in 1803.

Black emperor

In 1804, Saint-Domingue declared its independence as Haiti. Its first ruler, Jean-Jacques Dessalines, proclaimed himself Emperor Jacques I. He was assassinated in 1806. This was the beginning of a troubled history for Haiti. But it survived as an independent black-ruled state.

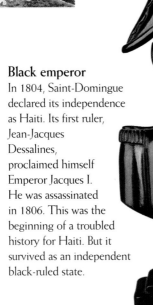

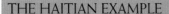

Jean-Baptiste Belley

Born in Senegal, West Africa, Jean-Baptise Belley was transported to Saint-Domingue as a slave in childhood. He fought in the uprising and, in 1793, was elected to represent the colony in the revolutionary assembly in Paris. There, his portrait was painted by artist Anne-Louis Girodet.

Many free black refugees from conflict-ridden Haiti settled in New Orleans.

THE HAITIAN EXAMPLE

The example of Haiti was used by both pro- and anti-slavery groups elsewhere in the world. To many black people, the Haitian struggle was an inspiration, proving that the enslaved could liberate themselves and successfully govern their own country. But slave owners pointed to the extreme violence that was unleashed by the uprising as evidence for the cruel and violent nature of blacks. They used the decline of the Haitian economy as evidence for their conviction that ending slavery would not work.

"I am Toussaint Louverture, my name is perhaps
known to you. I have undertaken vengeance. I want
liberty and equality to reign… Unite yourselves to

SLAVERY ENDS IN THE BRITISH EMPIRE

ALTHOUGH BRITAIN BANNED the slave trade in 1807, slavery continued in the British Empire. Slave uprisings in British colonies were suppressed with a brutality that sickened many British people. In Britain itself, the abolitionist movement revived in the 1820s. Under pressure from public opinion, British parliament passed an abolition of slavery act in 1833. It awarded £20 million ($95 million) to slave owners in compensation for the loss of their "property," but gave nothing to the freed slaves for their suffering.

Rebellion in Barbados

In 1816, slaves in Barbados rebelled after a colonial assembly representing slave owners rejected reforms put forward by the British government. The uprising was bloodless, but was put down with great severity. Among the slave leaders killed was a man named Bussa, who is celebrated today by this powerful Emancipation Statue, also known as the "Bussa Statue," in St. Michael, Barbados.

Rumors fuel revolt

In 1823, there was a revolt in Britain's South American colony, Demerara (now Guyana). It was provoked by a rumor that Britain had abolished slavery there but that local slave owners were conspiring to evade the law. A slave called Quamina, a deacon at a church run by missionary John Smith, was one of the revolt's leaders. When the uprising failed, Quamina was hunted down and killed. Smith was arrested and died in prison.

Anti-slavery propaganda

The Anti-Slavery Society was founded in Britain in 1823. It drew up petitions that attracted thousands of signatures and spread the abolitionist message wherever it could—even printing anti-slavery verses on pitchers and other pottery.

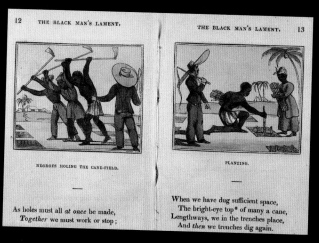

Stories of slavery

British anti-slavery campaigners directed their efforts at children as well as adults. *The Black Man's Lament* by Amelia Opie was an illustrated book of poems published in 1826. It told British children about the hard lives of slaves on a sugar plantation.

Jamaica's Baptist War

In 1831, Samuel Sharpe, a slave and Baptist preacher, organized a strike in Jamaica to press for freedom. The authorities responded brutally, and fighting followed. Fourteen whites were killed, but more than 500 blacks died in the suppression of the revolt, including Sharpe, who was hanged. Many Baptist and Methodist chapels were burned down in the aftermath of the revolt. Sam Sharpe's statue now stands in Montego Bay, Jamaica.

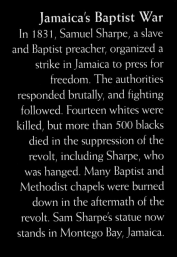

In 1833, more than 700,000 enslaved people were freed in the British Empire.

Proclamation of emancipation

Mounting pressure from the Anti-Slavery Society and slave revolts led the British parliament to pass a law ending slavery in the British Empire, with effect from 1834. But the law did not end slavery immediately. Freed slaves received no compensation for their sufferings and remained "apprenticed" to their owners until 1838. Even so, the proclamation was greeted with celebrations in the colonies.

COMPROMISE ON SLAVERY

IN THE EARLY 1800S, the United States had a balance between slave states in the South and free states—those that had abolished or were abolishing slavery—in the North. Most Northerners accepted that slavery in the Southern states was protected by the US Constitution and that the federal government had no right to interfere. But the US was expanding westward, and the question of whether slavery would be allowed in the western territories became a serious political problem. In 1819, the territory of Missouri applied for admission to the Union as a slave state. This exploded into a crisis that led to the brink of war.

Getting rich on cotton
The American South prospered in the first half of the 19th century. Enslaved workers increased as cotton production expanded to feed factories—mostly in Britain—making cloth. The South produced 60 per cent of the world's cotton, which was shipped from ports such as New Orleans.

Missouri Compromise, 1820–21

- Free states and territories
- Slave states and territories
- Open to slavery by Missouri Compromise
- Closed to slavery by Missouri Compromise
- Disputed territory

Maintaining the balance
The Missouri Compromise was intended to preserve the balance between slave states and free states. It admitted Maine as a free state on March 15 and Missouri as a slave state on August 10, 1821. But the Compromise forbade slavery in the Missouri Territory (formerly called the Louisiana Territory), north of the 36° 30′ latitude line, shown in red.

Northern factories

In the North, Americans were mostly farmers or craftsmen, but an industrial revolution was beginning, with large factories using water and later steam power. Workers were free—paid wages and hired or fired at will. Some Northern factories used cotton produced by enslaved labor in the South as their raw material.

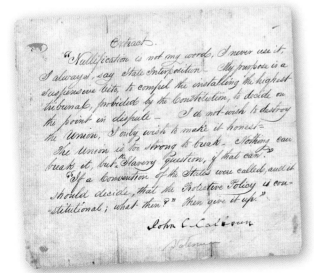

On the brink of war

Senator John C. Calhoun was a leading advocate of slavery and of states' rights. In 1833, his insistence on the right of South Carolina to nullify—or refuse to recognize—federal legislation brought the United States to the brink of civil war. Here, Calhoun writes that only "the slavery question" could break the Union.

The Missouri problem

In 1819, Congressman James Tallmadge proposed that Missouri should only become a state if it freed its slaves. This outraged pro-slavery Americans and there was talk of civil war. In the end, Missouri was admitted to the Union as a slave state, but it was agreed that no new slave states would be allowed north of Missouri's southern border.

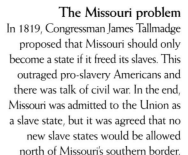

Jefferson's fears

The aged Thomas Jefferson was deeply alarmed by the Missouri crisis. He wrote that the controversy "like a fire bell in the night, awakened and filled me with terror." He believed the drawing of a line separating slave and free states would lead to a permanent division of the United States.

The four million slaves in the US were worth more than all the country's banks, railroads, and factories.

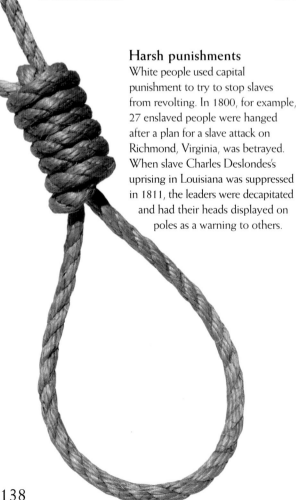

CLASS No. 1.			
Comprises those prisoners who were found guilty and executed.			
Prisoners Names.	Owners' Names.	Time of Commit.	How Disposed of.
Peter	James Poyas	June 18	
Ned	Gov. T. Bennett,	do.	Hanged on Tuesday
Rolla	do.	do.	the 2d July, 1822,
Batteau	do.	do.	on Blake's lands,
Denmark Vesey	A free black man	22	near Charleston.
Jessy	Thos. Blackwood	23	
John	Elias Horry	July 5	Do. on the Lines near
Gullah Jack	Paul Pritchard	do.	Ch.; Friday July 12.
Mingo	Wm. Harth	June 21	
Lot	Forrester	27	
Joe	P. L. Jore	July 6	
Julius	Thos. Forrest	8	
Tom	Mrs. Russell	10	
Smart	Robt. Anderson	do.	
John	John Robertson	11	
Robert	do.	do.	
Adam	do.	do.	
Polydore	Mrs. Faber	do.	Hanged on the Lines
Bacchus	Benj. Hammet	do.	near Charleston,
Dick	Wm. Sims	13	on Friday, 26th
Pharaoh	— Thompson	do.	July.
Jemmy	Mrs. Clement	18	
Mauidore	Mordecai Cohen	19	
Dean	— Mitchell	do.	
Jack	Mrs. Purcell	12	
Bellisle	Est. of Jos. Yates	18	
Naphur	do.	do.	
Adam	do.	do.	
Jacob	John S. Glen	16	
Charles	John Billings	18	
Jack	N. McNeill	22	
Cæsar	Miss Smith	do.	Do. Tues. July 30.
Jacob Stagg	Jacob Lankester	23	
Tom	Wm. M. Scott	24	
William	Mrs. Garner	Aug. 2	Do. Friday, Aug. 9.

AMERICAN UPRISINGS

SLAVE RESISTANCE WAS A DAILY REALITY and took many forms. Slaves would pretend to be sick, run away, destroy property, or even commit arson. In rare cases, slaves' resistance grew into large-scale revolts. But it was impossible for them to overcome the organized power of their owners when it came to a fight. Most white anti-slavery supporters were very critical if slaves used violence. The uprisings challenged what white people on both sides thought about slaves and increased the pressure for abolition.

The high price of liberty
Originally a slave in the West Indies, Denmark Vesey bought his freedom with lottery prize money. In 1822, he was accused of making plans for an uprising in South Carolina. The supposed plot was uncovered and 35 alleged conspirators were hanged. Vesey's name appears on this list of those executed.

Charles Deslondes's 1811 slave uprising in Louisiana was the largest in US history, with more than 200 slaves involved.

Harsh punishments
White people used capital punishment to try to stop slaves from revolting. In 1800, for example, 27 enslaved people were hanged after a plan for a slave attack on Richmond, Virginia, was betrayed. When slave Charles Deslondes's uprising in Louisiana was suppressed in 1811, the leaders were decapitated and had their heads displayed on poles as a warning to others.

Fight or flight
The futility of fighting slave owners led many of the enslaved to seek freedom by fleeing to the northern United States. Even there, however, slave owners pursued them using armed slave catchers, who would carry fugitives back into servitude.

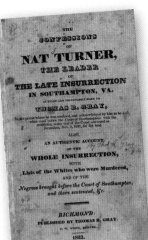

Nat Turner's uprising

The most famous slave rebellion was led by Nat Turner in Southampton County, Virginia, in 1831. Turner was an enslaved man of exceptional intelligence. According to his *Confessions*, dictated to a lawyer after the uprising, he experienced religious visions telling him to lead the enslaved in a "fight against the Serpent." It is reported that Turner and his followers killed around 60 white people before they were suppressed.

Turner captured

Nat Turner's uprising was crushed with extreme violence—many black people who took no part were killed. After six weeks on the run, Turner was seized at gunpoint, tried, and hanged.

Fighting the US army

Escaped slaves joined Seminoles—a Native American Tribe displaced from their land by white settlers—in resisting US forces in Florida. These "Black Seminoles" were excellent guerrilla fighters. In the Second Seminole War (1835–42), they won freedom, land, and military commissions as the price of peace.

"I had a vision—and I saw white spirits and black spirits engaged in battle, and the Sun was darkened—the thunder rolled in the heavens, and blood flowed in streams—and I heard a voice saying, 'Such is your luck… and let it come rough or smooth, you must surely bear it…'"

Nat Turner, The Confessions of Nat Turner, *interview in prison awaiting execution, 1831*

THE AMERICAN ABOLITIONISTS

FROM THE 1830s, A MOVEMENT campaigning for the total abolition of slavery gathered strength in the northern United States. White people took action, inspired by the idea that slavery contradicted the Christian faith and the founding principles of the United States. Free people of color, many of them former slaves, campaigned for the liberty of their enslaved brothers and sisters. There were divisions within the abolitionist movement over methods and goals. Anti-slavery campaigners faced varying degrees of hostility from many whites, even in the North, yet in the long run their influence was immense.

The state of Georgia offered a $5,000 reward for the arrest of abolitionist William Lloyd Garrison.

THE LIBERATOR COMMENCED JANUARY 1st 1831.

W.L.G.

"I am in earnest! I will not equivocate! I will not excuse! I will not retreat a single inch! And *I WILL BE HEARD!*"

William Lloyd Garrison
The first to publish the abolitionist journal *The Liberator* in 1831, Garrison played the leading role in founding the American Anti-Slavery Society. Unrelenting in his opposition to slavery, Garrison believed it could be ended through nonviolent means alone.

Frederick Douglass
The most prominent African-American abolitionist was Frederick Douglass, who had escaped from slavery at the age of 21. Douglass was a man of dignity and intelligence, and an inspired orator and writer. He believed that black people had to fight for their own freedom.

Sojourner Truth
Freed from slavery by emancipation in New York in 1827, Isabella Baumfree changed her name to Sojourner Truth after experiencing a religious calling to preach for abolition. An independent spirit with bitter experience of servitude, she also campaigned for women's rights.

Attacked by mobs

Abolitionists could not campaign in the southern states. They often faced violent attack even in the "free" North, where white workers feared abolition would threaten their jobs and racial privileges. In one incident in 1837, an armed mob attacked a warehouse in Alton, Illinois, in an effort to destroy a printing press belonging to anti-slavery journalist Elijah Lovejoy. Lovejoy was killed defending the building.

Lucretia Mott

A Quaker pacifist, Lucretia Mott campaigned for the emancipation of slaves and of women. She and other women were often discriminated against within the abolitionist movement. For example, women were denied seats at the 1841 World Anti-Slavery Convention.

Wendell Phillips

A wealthy Boston lawyer, Wendell Phillips quit the legal profession in 1836 to dedicate his life to the abolitionist cause. He was considered the movement's finest public speaker. A radical abolitionist, Phillips believed that the slave states should be expelled from the Union.

William Wells Brown

Born into slavery in Kentucky, William Brown escaped to freedom in the North. He worked on the Underground Railroad, helping other slaves escape to Canada, as well as campaigning tirelessly for the abolitionist cause. Brown was also a novelist, playwright, and historian.

"If there is no struggle, there is no progress. Those who profess to favor freedom, and deprecate [disapprove of] agitation, are men who want crops without plowing up the ground… Power concedes nothing without a demand. It never did and it never will."

Frederick Douglass, speaking at Canandaigua, New York, August 3, 1857

Fugitive Slave Law Convention, Cazenovia, New York, 1850; Frederick Douglass is seated to the left of the table

THE PROPAGANDA WAR

AMERICAN ABOLITIONISTS USED PROPAGANDA to try to persuade people that slavery was evil. They wrote sermons, songs, lectures, and pamphlets. Books such as the novel *Uncle Tom's Cabin* and the life stories of former slaves had a powerful impact, bringing home to Northerners the brutality to which the enslaved were subjected. Southern slave owners fought back, trying to project a positive image of plantation life and arguing that Southern slaves were better treated than industrial workers in the North.

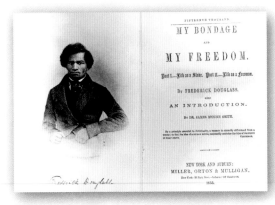

Slave narratives
The personal testimony of former slaves both drew attention to the evils of slavery and demonstrated the intelligence and dignity of the enslaved. Frederick Douglass wrote three autobiographies, of which *My Bondage and My Freedom* was the second.

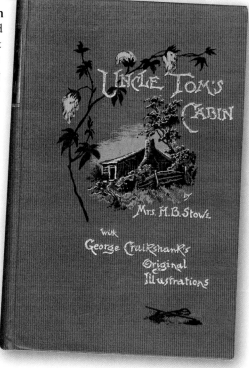

Uncle Tom's Cabin
The novel *Uncle Tom's Cabin*, published in 1852, was so successful that it was said to have outsold the Bible in the 1850s. Its dramatic, heart-breaking story of fugitives fleeing slavery and of the noble Uncle Tom's passive resistance to oppression appealed to the sentimentality of white Northerners.

Harriet Beecher Stowe
Uncle Tom's Cabin was the first adult novel by Connecticut-born Harriet Beecher Stowe. Criticized for its allegedly patronizing depiction of black people, it was at the time a radical and hugely influential work. President Lincoln is said to have called her "the little lady who made this big war."

Uncle Tom's Cabin was the best-selling novel in the world in the 19th century.

Capturing young minds

Abolitionists wanted to convince young children that slavery was evil. This jigsaw puzzle, intended for white children, shows enslaved black people kneeling gratefully to receive the gift of freedom from a white goddess.

Freedom song

Songs on anti-slavery themes were sung at abolitionist meetings, especially by the famous Hutchinson Family Singers. "The Fugitive's Song" was written by Jesse Hutchinson Jr., who also composed "Lincoln and Liberty."

An abolitionist meeting ends in violence

Public speeches and meetings were crucial to any political campaign in an age before radio and television. Abolitionist meetings were often violently disrupted by pro-slavery protestors.

Slavery justified

Virginian George Fitzhugh wrote influential pro-slavery tracts in the 1850s. He defended slavery partly on racist grounds, arguing that black people were incapable of benefiting from individual freedom and were only suited to brute labor. But he also attacked the free society of the North as treating its poorer workers worse than slaves.

The good life

Pro-slavery publications represented plantation life as happy and contented, with docile, childlike black people cared for by kindly owners, who were in turn respected and loved by their slaves. This pro-slavery cartoon was published in 1850.

VOICES
CALLS FOR FREEDOM

Abolitionists came from all sectors of society. There were African-Americans—former slaves—who spoke out over the cruelty suffered by enslaved people in the American South. Most white abolitionists were Christians who also advocated wider reforms for the moral improvement of society. Women, too, were involved in the abolitionist cause, and this involvement led directly to the first American campaign for women's voting rights.

"I COULD SEE that the all-wise creator had made man a free, moral, intelligent, and accountable being; capable of knowing good and evil. And I believed then, as I believe now, that every man has a right to wages for his labor; a right to his own wife and children; a right to liberty and the pursuit of happiness; and a right to worship God according to the dictates of his own conscience. But here, in the light of these truths, I was a slave, a prisoner for life; I could possess nothing, nor acquire anything but what must belong to my keeper. No one can imagine my feelings in my reflecting moments, but he who has himself been a slave…"

Born into slavery in Kentucky, Henry Bibb escaped to the North in 1842 and became an abolitionist campaigner, speaking with authority from his own experience. The testimony of former slaves was invaluable to the movement, because it disproved Southern claims that the enslaved were well-treated and contented.

"*SLAVE HOLDING AND slave holders must be rendered disreputable and odious. They must be stripped of their respectability and Christian reputation. They must be treated as men-stealers—guilty of the highest kind of theft, and sinners of the first rank... Honest men must be made to look upon their crimes with the same abhorrence and loathing, with which they regard the less guilty robber and assassin...*"

These words were written by abolitionist J. C. Hathaway as an introduction to William Wells Brown's account of his life under slavery and escape to freedom.

"*MY OBJECT HAS been to arouse you, as the wives and mothers, daughters and sisters, of the South, to a sense of your duty as women, and as Christian women, on that great subject, which has already shaken our country... and will continue mightily to shake it, until the polluted temples of slavery fall and crumble into ruin... Let them embody themselves in societies, and send petitions... entreating their husbands, fathers, brothers, and sons to abolish the institution of slavery; no longer to subject woman to the scourge and the chain, to mental darkness and moral degradation; no longer to tear husbands from their wives and children from their parents;... no longer to reduce American citizens to the abject condition of slaves.*"

Angelina Grimké was the daughter of a slave-owning judge in South Carolina. In defiance of her father, she became a Quaker and an abolitionist. Grimké wrote *An Appeal to the Christian Women of the South* in 1836. The tract was publicly burned in South Carolina.

THE UNDERGROUND RAILROAD

THE UNDERGROUND RAILROAD was a network of secret routes, supply points, and safe houses organized by abolitionists to help enslaved people escape from the Southern United States to freedom in the North, or across the border to Canada. The network was mostly run by free blacks, who worked at great personal risk as guides, or "conductors." In the 1840s and 1850s, the Underground Railroad helped some 30,000 people to escape slavery.

Dangerous journey
The most dangerous stretch of the Underground Railroad was through Southern territory. Small bands of runaways, led by a "conductor," kept far away from towns and villages. They crossed forests and swamps or mountain trails to escape detection by pursuing law officers, slave owners, or paid slave catchers. The runaways had to be fit and strong in order to survive the journey through this harsh terrain. Men often felt obliged to leave women and children behind on the plantation.

Courage and cunning
The desire for freedom led enslaved people to acts of great bravery and ingenuity. In 1848, Henry "Box" Brown had himself shipped in a crate from Richmond, Virginia, to Philadelphia. Those who assisted the enslaved were equally cunning. Dr. Alexander Milton Ross, an abolitionist from Belleville, Ontario, Canada, traveled through the South claiming to be studying bird life. But his real goal was to meet with slaves and organize their escape via the railroad.

A brave conductor and her passengers

Harriet Tubman (far left), herself an escaped slave, was the most famous of the "conductors" who secretly traveled into the South to act as guides for those wishing to escape. It was said that she "never lost a passenger."

In Canada, Quakers purchased 800 acres of land—the Wilberforce Settlement—for escaped slaves.

On track to freedom

The Underground Railroad was not literally a railroad. The organizers used railroad terms such as "passengers" for fugitives and "stations" for safe houses along the route as a simple sort of code. Escapees mostly traveled on foot or in horse-drawn carts. Carts with false bottoms were used to conceal fugitives being moved along the roads.

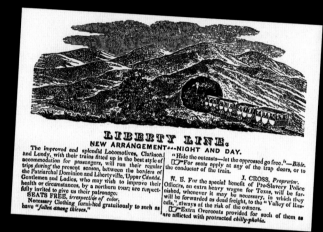

William Still

Born the son of a freed slave in New Jersey, William Still became a successful businessman and prominent abolitionist in Philadelphia. He helped organize systematic and large-scale aid for escaping slaves. One of the many fugitives whom he assisted turned out to be his own brother, who had been re-enslaved and separated from his family.

Hiding place

White sympathizers played an important part in the activities of the Underground Railroad. Many allowed their homes to be used as "stations," and created hiding places to conceal fugitive slaves. This crawl space, hidden by sliding shelves, can still be seen in the Dobbin House in Gettysburg, Pennsylvania.

Reaching Canada

Even after they arrived in a free state in the North, fugitive slaves were at risk of recapture, for they remained officially the property of their owners. The safest refuge was British-ruled Canada, where they could no longer be pursued by American slave catchers. Here, a party of runaways guided by Harriet Tubman is shown arriving at the Canadian border. Many assisted with settlement on arrival, such as former Maryland slave Josiah Henson. Reverend Henson helped found a school for refugee children, and his memoirs provided the inspiration for *Uncle Tom's Cabin* by Harriet Beecher Stowe.

FUGITIVES AND FREEDOM

THE FATE OF FUGITIVE SLAVES who had escaped from the slave South to non-slave states in the North became one of the great issues dividing the United States. The Fugitive Slave Act of 1850—a political triumph for the South—stated that the authorities in free states must cooperate with slave catchers in returning fugitives to their owners. Both free blacks and fugitives in the North found themselves at risk of being seized and carried South as slaves. After the Supreme Court ruling in the Dred Scott case in 1857, Northerners worried they might be powerless to prevent slavery from spreading to their states.

Determined pursuit
Southern slave owners were outraged by the fact that fugitives found refuge in the North. They were determined to get back their human property. Advertisements offering a reward for the recapture of escaped slaves were common. This poster gives a detailed description by the owner, Apos Tucker, of an African-American slave "about 30 years old, weighs about 160 pounds; high forehead with a scar on it…"

Slave catchers
Owners employed slave catchers to bring back fugitive slaves from free territory. Since slave catchers were paid for every black person they caught, they were often tempted to seize free people of color as well. Under the Fugitive Slave Act, it was almost impossible for African-Americans to assert their free status once in captivity. Slave catchers often used force in pursuit of their prey.

The 1850 Fugitive Slave law made it a crime to give shelter to an escaped slave.

Opposing slave catchers
Abolitionists held public meetings and protests in Northern cities against the activities of Southern slave catchers, who were denounced as "kidnappers."

Returned to slavery

Anthony Burns was a fugitive forcibly returned to his Southern owner from Boston in 1854. The case provoked mass protests. An armed guard had to prevent sympathizers from freeing Burns as he was marched to the ship that carried him back South. Abolitionists later bought Burns his freedom.

Dred and Harriet Scott

Dred Scott and his wife Harriet were enslaved people in Missouri. In 1846, they sued for the right to freedom, on the grounds that for many years their owner, an army surgeon, had held them in slave-free Illinois. Although the couple were were temporarily freed by a jury in 1850, the Missouri Supreme Court later ruled that they be returned to their masters. The case then arrived at the United States Supreme Court in 1856.

The Dred Scott decision

The Supreme Court in the 1850s was dominated by Southerners. Chief Justice Roger B. Taney, shown here, was aggressively pro-slavery. He found against Dred Scott, but did not stop there. He ruled that a black person could not be a citizen of the United States, and that Congress could not ban slavery from any state or territory. The decision caused uproar in the Northern states and was a major step toward the Civil War.

"As we traveled toward a land of liberty, my heart would at times leap for joy… The prospect of liberty before me, I was encouraged to press forward, my heart was strengthened, and I forgot that I was tired or hungry."

William Wells Brown describes his feelings as a fugitive slave in 1834, approaching freedom in Canada

A Ride for Liberty—The Fugitive Slaves by Eastman Johnson, c.1862, based on a scene witnessed in the Civil War

BLEEDING KANSAS

IN THE 1850S, THE EXPANDING United States was again plunged into crisis over slavery. The Kansas–Nebraska Act allowed territories to have a democratic vote to decide whether to join the Union as free or slave states. In Kansas this led to murderous clashes between pro- and anti-slavery groups. The fighting subsided and Kansas later joined the US as a free state. But John Brown, an abolitionist who had fought in Kansas, hatched a plot to liberate slaves throughout the American South by force of arms. Brown's failed attack on Harpers Ferry, Virginia, in 1859 left the US on the brink of civil war.

New territory
Kansas was declared a territory of the United States in 1854. Until then Native American land, it was to be opened up for American homesteaders to settle. This part of the country was thinly populated open spaces where there was, at the best of times, little by way of law and order.

Beecher's Bibles
In the lawless territory of Kansas, abolitionists were not afraid to take up arms. Abolitionist preacher Henry Ward Beecher raised money for Sharps rifles to be sent into Kansas to arm anti-slavery settlers. The rifles, known as "Beecher's Bibles," were used to fight the Border Ruffians, pro-slave bands from neighboring Missouri.

Overflowing violence
In 1856, massacre and counter-massacre by pro- and anti-slavery groups brought terror to small Kansas settlements. More than 50 people were killed. The violence overflowed into the US Congress, where South Carolina representative Preston Brooks beat and badly injured anti-slavery Massachusetts senator Charles Sumner as the debate over Kansas raged.

Fighting against slavery

John Brown was the aggressive leader of an anti-slavery fighting band in Kansas. He was responsible for the notorious Pottawatomie massacre in which five pro-slavers were hacked to death in cold blood. Later he led the brave defense of Osawatomie against a far superior force of Missouri armed raiders. Brown was sure that armed force could bring slavery to an end.

Ten of the 21 raiders were killed at Harpers Ferry, including two of Brown's sons.

Harpers Ferry Raid

With a band of 21 supporters—16 white and five black—John Brown launched an armed campaign in Virginia in October 1859. He planned to seize guns from the federal armory at Harpers Ferry, distribute them, and advance through the South, igniting an insurrection. But the plan failed. The raiders were trapped inside the armory, which was stormed by US Marines.

John Brown goes on trial

Captured at Harpers Ferry, Brown was found guilty of insurrection, treason, and murder, and hanged. His death turned Brown into an abolitionist martyr. Soon after the execution, a story circulated that on his way to the gallows, he had kissed a baby held up by a slave mother.

"LINCOLN BECOMES PRESIDENT"

BY THE 1850S, THE FUTURE OF SLAVERY was the central political issue in the United States. The Republican Party was formed in 1854 chiefly to oppose slavery's spread. In Abraham Lincoln, the Republicans found a candidate for the 1860 presidential election who was eloquent, brave, and honest. But Lincoln's anti-slavery opinions were unacceptable to the white South. He denied intending to force the Southern states to end slavery, but he did say that America could not "endure, permanently, half-slave and half-free." His election as president brought the divisions in the United States to breaking point.

Backwoods childhood
Born in this log cabin in Kentucky, Lincoln worked his way up from poverty to become a successful lawyer in Illinois. His experience made him believe every man should have the chance to prosper by his own efforts.

Slavery debated
Lincoln first became a nationally known politician when, in 1858, he engaged in a series of public debates with a pro-slavery Democrat named Stephen A. Douglas. These debates were widely reported in the press and Lincoln's powerful speeches made a big impression on both sides.

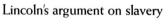

Lincoln's argument on slavery
In his debates with Douglas, Lincoln asserted that the founding principles of the Declaration of Independence applied to black people as well as white—that all men were created equal—and that slavery was tyrannical and immoral. While prepared to accept slavery where it already existed, he opposed its extension in the western territories. To many white Southerners he sounded like an anti-slavery extremist.

Debating race

Douglas believed in white superiority, calling blacks an "inferior and degraded race." Lincoln denied intending to make African-Americans the social and political equal of whites, knowing that this was totally unacceptable to white voters. But he insisted slavery was wrong and that its growth should be prevented. The Lincoln-Douglas debates are commemorated by a statue in Ottawa, Illinois.

A compromise candidate

The Republican National Convention met to select the party's presidential candidate in Chicago in May 1860. The politically inexperienced Lincoln arrived there with only an outside chance of selection, but he won the nomination as the compromise candidate most acceptable to opposing sections of the party.

Divisive election

In the presidential election itself, Lincoln was helped by divisions among his main opponents, the Democrats, who put up two rival candidates. This enabled him to become president with less than 40 percent of the popular vote and without winning a single slave state. South Carolina seceded (withdrew) from the Union even before Lincoln reached the White House.

Lincoln found national fame debating slavery with Douglas—a fame that helped him to the White House.

Opposing sides, 1861

Free states

Slave states

Territories

— Union and Confederate boundary

The states divided
Eleven Southern states seceded from the Union to form the Confederacy. Not all slave owners supported secession. The states of Maryland, Kentucky, Missouri, and Delaware, as well as the six westernmost counties of Virginia, fought on the Union side.

SECESSION AND CIVIL WAR

What the Union fought for
Most of those who fought on the Union side did so to preserve the United States. They saw their cause as patriotic and the Confederates as traitors—only a minority were inspired by anti-slavery sentiments.

AFTER LINCOLN WAS ELECTED president, 11 Southern states broke away from the Union. Lincoln was determined to resist this separation, but the newly formed Southern Confederacy stood firm and the two sides went to war. Superior in numbers and in industrial might, the Union defeated the Confederacy in May 1865. Lincoln did not fight the war to abolish slavery. He wrote in 1862, "If I could save the Union without freeing any slave I would do it, and if I could save it by freeing all the slaves I would do it." But the ending of slavery was a result of the war.

What the Confederacy fought for
The South claimed to be fighting for "states' rights"— the freedom of individual states to decide their own affairs. But they insisted on their right to secede from the Union—for recognition as an independent nation—in order to preserve slavery.

More than one in ten of all Union soldiers in the Civil War was African-American.

Heavy death toll
Some Civil War battles resulted in heavy losses. At Antietam in September 1862, there were more than 20,000 casualties in a single day. The three-day Battle of Gettysburg in July 1863 left some 50,000 men dead or wounded.

The president at Gettysburg
Lincoln (left of center, looking down) gave the Union cause dignity through his powerful address after the Battle of Gettysburg: "… that we here highly resolve that these dead shall not have died in vain… and that government of the people, by the people, for the people shall not perish from the earth."

Southern destruction
The war was mostly fought on Southern territory and brought devastation to the South. Supplies ran out as the Union cut off the Mississippi River and blockaded the coastline. Atlanta, Georgia, was burned to the ground and the Virginia capital Richmond was in ruins by the time of the Confederate surrender in 1865.

NEW YORK DRAFT RIOTS

In 1863, Irish immigrants in New York City rioted in protest at being drafted into the Union army. The riots, among the most violent in US history, developed into murderous assaults on African-Americans. These racist attacks expressed the resentment of some white people at the idea of fighting a war for the benefit of black people.

AFRICAN-AMERICANS IN THE CIVIL WAR

Fleeing to Union lines in the North
Thousands of the enslaved fled the South, seeking freedom with the Northern armies. Labeled "contrabands," the fugitives often met an unfriendly reception and, until spring 1862, were sometimes even returned to their owners.

THE AMERICAN CIVIL WAR started as a conflict between white Americans, but African-Americans seized the chance to fight for their freedom. At first, black people offering to fight for the North met only rejection and suspicion. Lincoln was worried that enrolling African-Americans would alienate those on the Union side who were opposed to abolishing slavery. But as the war became more desperate, the North enrolled black volunteers, first in support roles but later as combat troops.

By the end of the war, 180,000 African-Americans had fought for their freedom—about one-third of them died in the struggle.

Men of Color, To Arms!
Abolitionist Frederick Douglass urged African-Americans to join black regiments, declaring, "Liberty won only by white men would lose half its luster." Douglass acted as an adviser to President Lincoln during the conflict, arguing for better conditions and pay for black soldiers. He believed that the abolition of slavery should be the ultimate goal of the war.

Courage under fire
One of the first African-American volunteer regiments was the 54th Massachusetts. In July 1863, the regiment attacked the defenses of Fort Wagner at Charleston harbor, South Carolina. They lost 330 men to the Confederates' 12. The assault was a military failure but a moral victory, proving the courage of African-American soldiers.

Abolitionist commander
Black troops usually fought under white officers. Colonel Robert Shaw, an abolitionist, lost his life leading the 54th Massachusetts at Fort Wagner. He is commemorated, together with his regiment, on this bronze monument in Boston.

Medal of Honor
Twenty-three African-American soldiers and sailors received the Medal of Honor for "conspicious gallantry" during the Civil War. Of these, 14 went to members of 4th US Colored Troops for their part in the battle of New Market Heights, Virginia, in which 850 Union soldiers were killed.

First black officer
Abolitionist Martin Delany campaigned for the formation of an African-American army, which he planned to lead in an invasion of the South. This did not happen, but Lincoln had Delany appointed the first black officer in the US Army.

Hard-won pride
Serving in racially segregated units, black troops suffered unequal treatment over promotion and pay. If captured by Southerners—who refused to recognize them as combatants—they were tortured and massacred. After the war, many black troops were resettled as free men in Florida, Nova Scotia in Canada, and in England.

"Through the cannon-smoke of that black night the manhood of the colored race shines before many eyes that would not see, rings in many ears that would not hear, wins many hearts that would not hitherto believe."

Author and abolitionist Louisa May Alcott, author of Little Women, writing in Atlantic Monthly, November 1863

Black troops of the 54th Massachusetts Regiment during the assault of Fort Wagner, South Carolina, July 18, 1863

EMANCIPATION PROCLAIMED

IN JANUARY 1863, WITH CIVIL WAR RAGING, President Lincoln issued the Emancipation Proclamation, declaring all enslaved people under Confederate control "forever free of their servitude." The immediate goal of the proclamation was to undermine the Southern war effort, and it was limited in its genuine power to make Confederate slaves free. But the proclamation ensured that a Union victory in the war would end slavery in the South. An amendment, or change, to the Constitution banning slavery in the US was ratified (approved) in 1865.

Celebrating freedom
The Emancipation Proclamation was seen by abolitionists as a mighty victory. When the proclamation became effective on January 1, 1863, white abolitionists and African-American soldiers joined in flag-waving parades.

President under pressure
Lincoln maintained his commitment to emancipation in the face of bitter attacks from those supporting the Union side in the war who opposed the abolition of slavery. His victory in the presidential election in 1864, however, showed that opinion in the North had swung sharply in favor of abolition.

Thirteenth Amendment
In early 1865, a proposed Amendment of the US Constitution abolishing slavery was passed by the US Congress and signed by President Lincoln, who submitted it to the states for ratification (approval). Declaring that "Neither slavery nor involuntary servitude... shall exist within the United States," the Amendment was formally adopted in December 1865, eight months after the end of the Civil War.

Greeted with joy
Shortly after Richmond, the Confederate capital, fell to
Union troops in April 1865, Lincoln visited the city. He
was surrounded by crowds of jubilant African-Americans
who greeted him with enthusiasm.

Death of a president
Lincoln was assassinated by Confederate sympathizer
John Wilkes Booth on April 14, 1865, five days after the
end of the war. Booth's action was provoked by a speech
in which Lincoln supported voting rights for freed slaves.
Lincoln's death deprived the United States of its most
important leader at a time when the nation was beginning
the difficult task of rebuilding the Southern states.

*Lincoln said, "In
giving freedom to
the slave, we assure
freedom to the free."*

The road to citizenship
For black Americans, there was universal
relief at the ending of slavery, despite
the problems of poverty and racial
prejudice that lay ahead. The right to
vote was granted in 1870, and this act
of citizenship was a proud experience
for those so long held in bondage.

VOICES GLAD TO BE FREE

Individual African-Americans experienced the ending of slavery at different times. Most achieved freedom during the Civil War, while some were only liberated after the war's end. Naturally, their response was one of joy and relief. White Americans were far more varied in their reactions, but in the North, at least, it was accepted that the ending of slavery was inevitable.

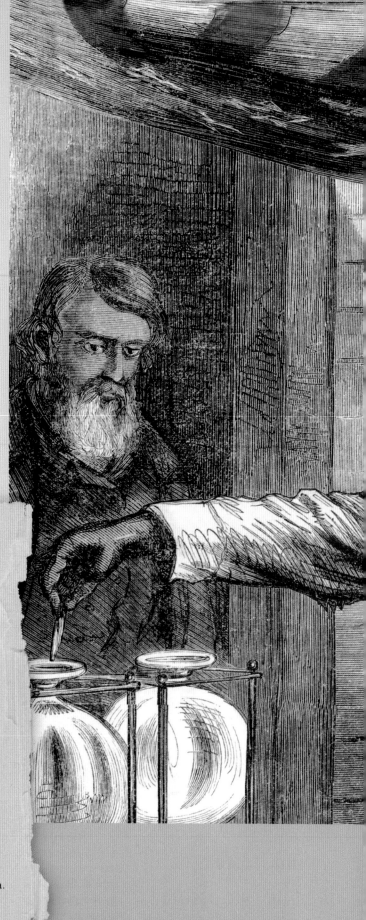

"AS THE GREAT day grew nearer, there was more singing in the slave quarters than usual. It was bolder, had more ring, and lasted later into the night. Most of the verses of the plantation songs had some reference to freedom... Some man who seemed to be a stranger (a United States officer, I presume) made a little speech and then read a rather long paper—the Emancipation Proclamation, I think. After the reading we were told that we were all free, and could go when and where we pleased. My mother, who was standing by my side, leaned over and kissed her children, while tears of joy ran down her cheeks."

Booker T. Washington was born into slavery in Virginia. He was nine years old when emancipation was declared, and described his memory of the event in his autobiography *Up From Slavery*, published in 1901. Washington became a distinguished educator and spokesman in the post-slavery era.

"**M**Y DEAR WIFE, It is with great joy I take this time to let you know where I am. I am now in safety in the 14th Regiment of Brooklyn. This day I can address you, thank God, as a free man. I had a little trouble in getting away. But as the Lord led the children of Israel to the land of Canaan, so he led us to a land where freedom will reign in spite of earth and hell. Dear, you must make yourself content that I am free from all the slaver's lash..."

John Boston was an enslaved man from Maryland. He wrote this letter in January 1862, after escaping to the Union army. He was among many thousands of enslaved African-Americans who freed themselves during the Civil War.

"**I**F THEY [black soldiers and sailors] stake their lives for us, they must be prompted by the strongest motive—even the promise of freedom. And the promise being made, must be kept... Why should they give their lives for us, with full notice of our purpose to betray them?... There have been men who have proposed to me to return to slavery the black warriors... I should be damned in time and in eternity for so doing. The world shall know that I will keep my faith to friends and enemies, come what will."

President Abraham Lincoln produced this reply to people who criticized his policy toward slavery in August 1864. Like many white people in the North, Lincoln felt that the contribution of African-American troops to the Civil War gave them the right to freedom.

Independence and freedom
The issue of slavery in Cuba became entangled with the question of Cuban independence from Spain. Enslaved black people fought on both sides in a war that lasted ten years, between those for and against independence; those for independence lost. When the war ended in 1878, all slaves who had taken part in the fighting were freed.

ABOLITION IN BRAZIL AND CUBA

THE ABOLITION OF SLAVERY in the United States in 1865 left Brazil and the Spanish colony of Cuba as the last two major slave-owning societies in the Americas. Both had slave-based economies that had expanded rapidly through the 19th century, using illegally imported slaves from Africa. But the Brazilian and Spanish authorities came under pressure from the US to end slavery. They also faced resistance from their enslaved communities. Spain finally abolished slavery in Cuba in 1886. In Brazil, the Law of the Free Womb of 1871—which freed children born to slave mothers after that date—was followed by total abolition in 1888.

Slavery continues in Brazil

When most of the countries of Central and South America won independence in the early 1800s, the former Spanish colonies abolished slavery. Cuba, which remained a Spanish colony until 1898, did not abolish slavery until 1886. Brazil, formerly a Portuguese colony, kept slavery and expanded it. This image of Brazilian plantation life dates from 1857.

In the mid-19th century, Brazil imported some 60,000 enslaved Africans every year.

Bitter harvest

In the 19th century, a boom in coffee production meant that work on coffee plantations became the most important use of slave labor in Brazil. But, by the 1880s, the majority of the 750,000 enslaved Brazilians became increasingly resistant to authority. Thousands began to desert the plantations in search of freedom, helped by the army's unwillingness to round them up.

Free at last

On May 13, 1888, the *Lei Áurea* ("Golden Law") decreed the total abolition of slavery in Brazil. The *Lei Áurea* was signed by Brazil's Princess Isabel, acting in place of her father, Emperor Pedro II, who was away in Europe. Abolition was greeted with mass celebrations in major cities.

Plantation-owners' revenge

Not everyone was pleased to see slavery end in Brazil. Plantation owners were outraged at the loss of their human property—no compensation was paid to slave owners, or to freed slaves. Rich landowners overthrew Emperor Pedro II the following year, making Brazil a republic. The Emperor died in exile.

AFTERMATH OF SLAVERY

BY 1888, SLAVERY HAD BEEN abolished everywhere in the Americas, but it cast a long shadow over the years that followed. The enslaved were freed into societies where economic and political power still rested with whites, and systematic racism ensured that black people were kept at the bottom of the pile. Although emancipation was the end of one struggle, it was the beginning of another—the long struggle for racial equality and for full human and political rights.

Silent monument to oppression
Throughout the South, enslaved people lived in tiny huts like these which form part of a double row of 22 slave cabins at Evergreen Plantation in Louisiana. Hidden behind the owners' white-pillared mansion, these cabins are some of the few that still remain today.

The 15th Amendment to the US Constitution guarantees former male slaves the right to vote

The US Supreme Court rules racial segregation acceptable if facilities are "separate but equal"

President Roosevelt orders equal employment of races in US defense industries

US Supreme Court denies citizenship to slaves, former slaves, and their descendants

The end of the period of Reconstruction leaves whites in control of the US Southern states

The National Association for the Advancement of Colored People founded in the US

President Truman orders an end to racial segregation in US armed forces

| 1857 | 1868 | 1870 | 1877 | 1890–1908 | 1896 | 1909 | 1925 | 1941 | 1948 |

The 14th Amendment to the US Constitution promises former slaves full rights as citizens

Southern state governments in US pass laws imposing racial segregation and stripping blacks of the right to vote

The white racist Ku Klux Klan claims 5 million members across the US

The United Nations Universal Declaration of Human Rights outlaws slavery worldwide

Decolonization in the West Indies
begins: Jamaica and Trinidad are
independent of Britain

The TV mini-series *Roots* stimulates
African-American interest in their
enslaved past

The US Supreme Court
declares racially segregated
education unconstitutional

The Civil Rights Act and the
Voting Rights Act are passed in
the United States

The United Nations declares
a year of commemoration
of slavery

| 1954 | 1955 | 1962 | 1963 | 1964–65 | 1968 | 1977 | 2001 | 2004 | 2008 |

The Montgomery Bus Boycott
begins direct action against
segregation in US South

Martin Luther King Jr. leads
the March on Washington
demanding civil rights

Martin Luther King Jr.
assassinated; race riots in
more than 100 US cities

World Conference on Racism sees
demands for reparations payments
for slaves' descendants

An African-American is
elected US president

Farming for themselves
In Jamaica, rather than labor for wages on the plantations, former slaves preferred to become small farmers. Working a piece of their own land gave only a poor income, but allowed them to lead fully independent lives. These Jamaicans are carrying bananas for export.

Finding fresh labor
Deserted by their former slaves, many plantation owners in the Caribbean found a new source of labor in "coolies" imported from Asia. These were indentured workers, mostly recruited in India, who bound themselves to work for a certain period of time. The living and working conditions of Indians, such as these people in Jamaica, were often little better than slavery.

LIFE AFTER SLAVERY

WHEN SLAVERY WAS ABOLISHED, black people in the Americas did not receive any financial compensation or land grants to help them prosper in freedom. Instead, they were held back by racial discrimination and segregation. After years of working in gangs under white supervision, they wanted independence and control over their own lives. But former slave owners were still in possession of the land, ensuring that the formerly enslaved remained economically dependent on them. Freedom from enslavement was a major gain, but poverty and injustice remained the lot of most.

Life as a sharecropper
In the Southern United States, many formerly enslaved people became sharecroppers. The former slave owner let the former slave have a parcel of land to work, often also providing seed and a mule. In return, the sharecropper agreed to give a portion of the crop— generally half—to the owner at harvest. In practice, sharecropping ensured that black people in the South remained impoverished and were usually tied to the landowner by debts they could not pay off.

Dark poverty

Brazil never adopted racial segregation to the degree practiced in the United States. As a result, Brazilians developed every shade of skin color as people of African and non-African origin mixed and married. But even in Brazil, the darker the shade of a person's skin, the more likely he or she was to end up living in poverty.

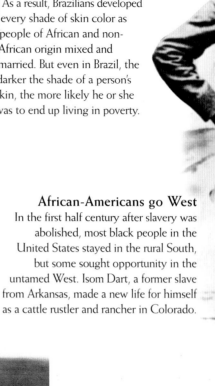

In 1900, an average African-American in the US South earned under $1 a day.

African-Americans go West

In the first half century after slavery was abolished, most black people in the United States stayed in the rural South, but some sought opportunity in the untamed West. Isom Dart, a former slave from Arkansas, made a new life for himself as a cattle rustler and rancher in Colorado.

Making a new world

In the face of white racism, free blacks created their own cultural world. They founded new churches and Christian schools, and created their own festivals, music, and customs. These churchgoers were photographed in the United States at the end of the 19th century.

RECONSTRUCTION AND RACISM

IN THE UNITED STATES, the Civil War was followed by bitter political struggles over former slaves' place in society. The 13th, 14th, and 15th Amendments to the US Constitution guaranteed African-Americans freedom, full citizenship, and the right to vote. During this period, called Reconstruction, former slaves briefly enjoyed full citizenship. Reconstruction ended in 1877 in the face of violent white resistance. In the years after 1877, black people in the South lost civil and political rights, including the right to vote, and were subject to strict racial segregation.

Rebuilding the South
Black politicians played an important part in the Reconstruction of the Southern states after the Civil War. Oscar Dunn, once an escaped slave, was elected lieutenant-governor of Louisiana. There were 29 African-American representatives at the convention gathered to draw up a new Louisiana state constitution in 1868.

African-American senator
Hiram Rhodes Revels, a pastor in the African Methodist Episcopal church, became the first African-American senator in 1870. He represented Mississipi and was one of two black senators in the Reconstruction era, before Southern whites stopped African-Americans from holding office. The next black senator was not elected

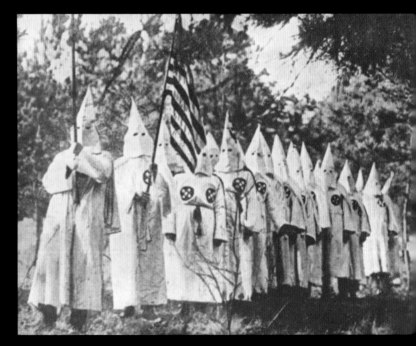

Racist reaction
White movements in the Southern states reacted to the ending of slavery by asserting racial supremacy. The hooded Ku Klux Klan was the most notorious of these organizations. Originally a group of former Confederate soldiers, they believed whites to be the dominant race, and attacked and murdered free blacks. The group underwent a revival in the 1920s, achieving a large membership.

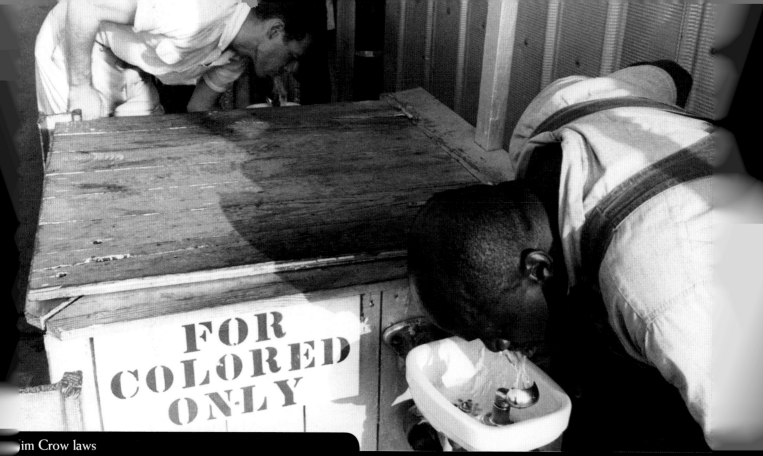

Jim Crow laws

By 1900, Southern states were adopting "Jim Crow" laws (named after a character on the stage). These laws imposed racial segregation in schools, transportation, washrooms, eating places, and theaters. Through means such as literacy tests, black people were denied the right to vote. This denial, or disfranchisement, was approved by the US Supreme Court.

In the 1890s, more than 1,000 African-Americans were murdered by lynch mobs, most in the South.

Women fight back

A teacher whose parents had been slaves, Ida B. Wells became one of the first protesters against segregation when, in 1883, she refused to give up her seat in a whites-only car on a train in Tennessee. Wells campaigned against lynching and was active in promoting both women's rights and black civil rights.

POST-SLAVERY EDUCATOR

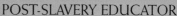

The most prominent and influential black leader of the early post-slavery era in the United States was Booker T. Washington. He paid for his own schooling by undertaking a series of menial jobs, rising to become a teacher at the Hampton Institute in Virginia. Judging white power and prejudice too strong to be attacked head on, he encouraged African-Americans to improve their lives as best they could in the face of segregation. As head of the Tuskegee Institute in Alabama, founded in 1881, he promoted "industrial education," which emphasized instruction in trades, agriculture, and other practical pursuits.

Reign of terror

The use of extreme violence, including murder by lynching, to intimidate black people became a feature of life in the Southern states. This image from 1874 suggests that the fate of African-Americans terrorized by white racist groups was worse than slavery.

THE FREEDOM STRUGGLE CONTINUES

IN THE 20TH CENTURY, the struggle to overcome slavery's legacy of injustice and racism continued. In the Caribbean, where most islands were ruled by Europeans as colonies, the black majority struggled for independence. In the United States, the African-American minority fought for civil rights and an end to discrimination, often in the face of violent intimidation. Although many victories were won, people of African origin remain victims of poverty and inequality in the 21st century in many parts of the Americas.

Black nationalism
One response to white racism was black separatism—the idea that black people should live separately from whites. In the early 20th century, Jamaican Marcus Garvey supported this view, and was active in the Back to Africa movement.

Civil Rights Movement

In contrast to black separatism, civil rights campaigners in the US fought for the full integration of African-Americans into American society. In the 1950s and 1960s, black activists met a violent response in the South as they defied segregation and asserted the rights of black people to vote.

Non-violent protest played a large part in the struggle for black civil rights.

Campaign success

Rosa Parks (center) triggered a boycott of segregated buses in Montgomery, Alabama, in 1955 by refusing to give up her seat for a white person. A lifelong civil rights activist, Parks lived to see the achievement of many of the goals of the movement, including desegregation and voting rights for African-Americans.

Martin Luther King Jr.

The most prominent leader of the Civil Rights Movement in the 1950s and 1960s was Martin Luther King Jr. Addressing a march on Washington, D.C., in 1963, he expressed his vision of a racially integrated society in his "I have a dream" speech. King was assassinated in 1968.

High achievers

By the 21st century, some African-Americans had achieved great professional success, showing the distance traveled by the United States since the days of slavery. The election of Barack Obama as president in 2008 was striking evidence of how far the country had come from the 1950s, when most black people were not even allowed to vote.

CARIBBEAN INDEPENDENCE

In the 1940s, the French-ruled Caribbean islands of Martinique and Guadeloupe became French departments (administrative divisions, similar to counties), electing deputies to the French parliament. Most of the British-ruled islands became independent in the1960s—Jamaica and Trinidad in 1962, and Barbados and Guyana in 1966. The descendants of the enslaved at last ruled the islands to which their ancestors had been transported. Independence in Jamaica was celebrated with music and parades.

Poverty trap

Since the 1960s, increasing numbers of African-Americans have achieved a comfortable standard of living and social status, but many remained trapped in poverty, facing problems such as low educational standards and high crime rates. These children were photographed in the Bronx in 1971.

SLAVERY AND MEMORY

WAYS OF REMEMBERING SLAVERY changed over time. In the first half of the 20th century, there was a tendency to romanticize the slave past, ignoring its horrors and injustices. A renewed awareness of slave origins was part of the upsurge of black consciousness starting in the 1960s. For black people, this brought both anger at the injustices of the past and an eagerness to reconnect with African roots. White people were forced to confront one of the most shameful episodes in their history.

Roots received the highest-ever ratings for a TV mini series. More than 100 million watched the last episode.

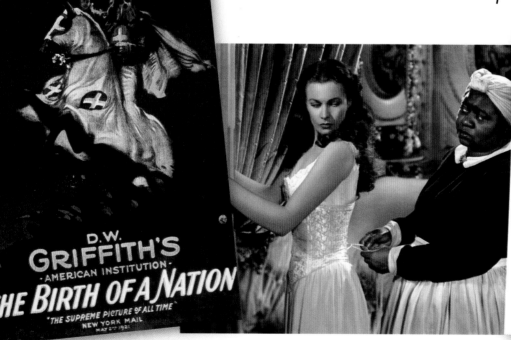

The Birth of a Nation
A movie considered the first masterpiece of American cinema, *The Birth of a Nation* celebrated slavery as being good for the enslaved, and represented the Ku Klux Klan as heroes. When it was first shown in 1915, it provoked protests by African-Americans and riots by white mobs.

Gone With the Wind
The best-selling novel *Gone With the Wind* by Margaret Mitchell, made into an Oscar-winning movie in 1939, presented a glamorized view of plantation life in the pre-Civil War South. It falsely suggested that the enslaved usually loved and respected their owners.

Alex Haley's Roots
The book and TV series *Roots* had immense impact in the 1970s. Imaginatively tracing author Alex Haley's family origins back to Africa, it was the first real attempt by mainstream American culture to come to grips with the reality of slavery and the slave trade.

Slavery museums

Many new museums designed to pass on knowledge of the slave trade and slavery to future generations opened in the first decade of the 21st century. These children are visiting the National Underground Railroad Freedom Center in Cincinnati, Ohio, opened in 2004.

The rise of Roots tourism

The success of the TV series *Roots* was partly responsible for the new phenomenon of slavery tourism from the 1980s. African-Americans began traveling to West Africa to visit sites associated with the slave trade, such as Gorée Island near the city of Dakar, Senegal, above. There was also a new interest in tracing family history back to slave origins.

Search for reparations

New awareness of the slave past led to demands for reparations (compensation) to be paid to descendants of the enslaved. This view was discussed at the World Conference Against Racism in Durban in 2001, opened by Kofi Annan, then UN Secretary-General. Some Western governments expressed regret for slavery, but all rejected claims for compensation.

VOICES
LEGACY OF SLAVERY

Many descendants of enslaved Africans have struggled to come to terms with their ancestral past. Some have preferred to dismiss the past as a thing to be forgotten, looking only to the future. But others have found strength in identifying with victims of past wrongs, and in exploring their origins. While anger and sorrow have been natural responses, black people have also enriched their lives by grounding themselves in history.

"*I HAVE LONG since ceased to cherish any spirit of bitterness against the Southern white people on account of the enslavement of my race… When we rid ourselves of prejudice, or racial feeling, and look facts in the face, we must acknowledge that, notwithstanding the cruelty and moral wrong of slavery, the ten million Negroes inhabiting this country, who themselves or whose ancestors went through the school of American slavery, are in a stronger and more hopeful condition, materially, intellectually, morally, and religiously, than is true of an equal number of black people in any other portion of the globe.*"

Born in 1856, Booker T. Washington became an educator in the post-emancipation era. In his autobiography *Up From Slavery*, he made it clear that he did not condone enslavement, saying that he had never met a person "who did not want to be free." But he did believe that America offered black people the best chance of self-improvement.

"SO WE'RE ALL black people, so-called Negroes, second-class citizens, ex-slaves. You're nothing but an ex-slave. You don't like to be told that. But what else are you? You are ex-slaves. You didn't come here on the Mayflower. You came here on a slave ship. In chains, like a horse, or a cow, or a chicken. And you were brought here by the people who came here on the Mayflower, you were brought here by the so-called Pilgrims, or Founding Fathers. They were the ones who brought you here... And what we have foremost in common is that enemy—the white man."

Born in 1925, Malcolm X emerged in the early 1960s as an eloquent campaigner for justice and black pride. He rejected integration as a social goal and expressed the anger of young African-Americans at the injustices to which their people had been subjected. This is an excerpt from a speech he made to an all-black audience in 1963. Malcolm X was assassinated in 1965.

"THIRTY YEARS AGO I was an 11-year-old growing up in West London. One evening I sat down with my family to watch a new television program called Roots. It was a moment that changed my life. By the end of the series I had told my mother that I would one day trace my heritage back to Africa and reclaim an ancestral name. Before I watched the program I was called Ian Roberts, but now my name is Kwame Kwei-Armah... What made Roots so difficult for many people with Caribbean heritage was that it confronted them with the fact that their families originally came from Africa... We felt no kinship with Africa. But Roots changed the way British West Indians thought about themselves..."

Actor and playwright Kwame Kwei-Armah was born in Britain in 1967. His parents were immigrants from Grenada. His story shows how, until quite recently, most West Indians had little awareness of their African roots and the enslavement of their ancestors.

Slavery in Africa
In African countries such as Mauritania, Niger, Chad, Mali, and Sudan, many thousands of people are still exploited as slaves, forced to work without pay and liable to be sold as property. Most children in these regions have to work.

SLAVERY TODAY

TODAY, SLAVERY AND SLAVE TRADING are illegal in international law and in the laws of every nation of the world. Yet the United Nations estimates that 20 million people continue to be enslaved worldwide. These people, many of them children, may be in bondage to an owner, physically abused and intimidated by the threat of violence. Many enslaved people are trafficked from country to country, just as people were during the centuries of the transatlantic slave trade.

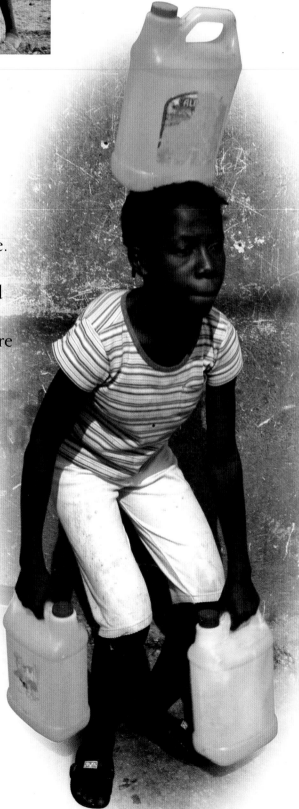

Haitian child slavery
Sadly Haiti, site of the famous slave rebellion of the early 19th century, has one of the worst problems with child slavery. About 300,000 Haitian children are "restaveks," handed over to well-off city dwellers by their impoverished parents to work as domestic slaves. Restaveks are often abused and badly fed.

Rug-makers of Pakistan
South Asia has more unfree workers than anywhere else. They are "bonded laborers" whose family owes a debt they cannot repay. As a result they are forced to work for their creditor for nothing. Pakistan's carpet industry is notorious for using children as bonded labor.

Debt slavery in the Amazon

In Brazil, laborers are recruited from the poorest areas of the country to work in the Amazon rain forest. Once there, they are made to fall into debt to their employers—debt they can never repay on their pitiful wages. As a result, they are forced to work permanently for the employer, who takes all their income.

Exploiting illegal immigrants

Many thousands of illegal immigrants are brought into the United States, Britain, and other countries with advanced economies from poorer parts of the world. They are trafficked in appalling conditions and, once they reach their destination, they are often subject to extreme exploitation.

By some estimates, around eight million children are victims of slavery around the world today.

Universal condemnation

By the 21st century, slavery and slave trading, past and present, were condemned by all. Here, Britain's Queen Elizabeth II lays a wreath to commemorate victims of the slave trade on the 200th anniversary of abolition of the trade in 2007.

No more auction block for me,
No more, no more,
No more auction block for me,
Many thousands gone.

No more driver's lash for me,
No more, no more,
No more driver's lash for me,
Many thousands gone.

Slave spiritual song

At Anse Cafard Slave Memorial, Martinique, the 20 white stone statues, which face toward Africa, commemorate those slaves lost in a shipwreck in 1830

Abolition
The banning of slavery, or the slave trade.

Abolitionist
A person who believes in banning slavery and the slave trade.

Americas
The continents of North and South America, including the islands of the West Indies.

Baptists
Members of Christian groups practicing adult baptism, often by immersion in a lake or river.

Barracoons
A barracks in which enslaved peoples were formerly held in temporary confinement.

Branded
Marked permanently with a hot iron, and used on some enslaved people to denote ownership.

Caribbean
The West Indies and the countries around the Caribbean Sea.

Civil rights
The rights of an individual citizen, such as the right to vote and the right to equal treatment regardless of race or gender.

Coffle
A line of enslaved people chained together for transporting across country.

Colonies
Countries ruled by other countries as part of their empire, or European settlements in the Americas.

Colored
Term once used for people who are either black, or of mixed race—for example, with one black and one white parent.

Confederate
Term describing the 11 states on the Southern side in the Civil War that seceded from the Union.

Emancipation
Term used for the freeing of slaves on a large scale.

Empire
A large area of the world ruled by a single country or person.

Enlightenment
A movement of thought in the 18th century that criticized existing customs and traditions and sought to create a better world based on rational principles.

Enslaved African/Enslaved person
A servant without freedom and personal rights, or one who is the property of another whether by capture, purchase, or birth.

Factory
In the slave trade, a European fort or trading base on the African coast; more usually, a term for a place where goods are mass-produced using machinery.

Field slave
An enslaved person who worked on a plantation.

Founding Fathers
Term used for the political leaders who founded the United States and established its Constitution.

Free person of color
Term once used for any black or mixed-race person who was not enslaved.

Free state
Term used in the 19th century for states of the United States that had abolished, or were in the process of abolishing, slavery.

Fugitive
An escaped slave, especially one seeking refuge in the free states of the United States and Canada.

House slave
An enslaved person who worked as a domestic servant rather than in the fields.

Human rights
Freedoms that all people should have the right to enjoy.

Indentured
Term used for people who were tied to work for a master for a fixed period of years.

Insurrection
A rebellion against authority, for example, an attempt by enslaved people to take over a slave ship.

Jim Crow laws
Laws introduced in the southern United States, mostly from the 1890s, creating racial segregation and denying basic rights to African-Americans.

Ku Klux Klan
An American organization devoted to maintaining white dominance over other ethnic groups.

Manumission
The voluntary freeing of individual slaves by their owners.

...Escaped slaves living in remote areas of West Indian islands.

Methodists
Christians belonging to a movement originally inspired by John Wesley in the 18th century.

Middle Passage
Term used for the crossing of the Atlantic by slave ships from Africa to the Americas.

Missionary
A person sent to educate others about a religious faith.

Monopoly
The exclusive right to trade certain goods.

New World
The Americas, as opposed to the "Old World" of Africa, Asia, and Europe.

Overseer
A person in charge of enslaved workers on a plantation.

Outward Passage
Term used for the first stage in the transatlantic slave trade, with ships carrying goods from Europe to trade in Africa for captured Africans.

Plantation
A large estate mostly growing a single crop such as sugar cane, tobacco, or cotton.

Pro-slavery
Describes a person, an action, or an idea that is in favor of slavery.

Quakers
Christian sect that was prominent in anti-slavery campaigns in the 18th century.

Racial discrimination
The unfair treatment of people of a certain racial group.

Racism
The belief that some people are naturally superior to others because of the racial group they belong to.

Rebellion
Organized armed resistance against established government or authority.

...The period after the Civil War in the United States, from 1865 to 1877, when the government began the process of restoring the seceding Southern states to the rights and privileges of the Union.

Reparation payment
Owed to some person or group in compensation for sufferings or exploitation they have suffered.

Return Passage
The third stage in the transatlantic slave trade with ships carrying items grown or made in the Caribbean or the Americas.

Revolt
An uprising against a ruler or government, sometimes including going over to a rival power.

Runaway
Another word for a fugitive—an enslaved person who has escaped from his or her owner.

Secession
The withdrawal of states from the United States at the start of the Civil War.

Segregation system
A system under which non-whites were denied access to schools, transportation facilities, eating places, housing, and places of entertainment reserved for whites.

Serf
In European history, a person who was tied to the land on which they worked.

Slave
A person who has had his or her freedom taken away, becoming the property of another person.

Slave driver
An enslaved person put in charge of other slaves, entrusted with making them work hard.

Slave state
Term used in the 19th century for states of the United States in which slavery was legal.

State
An administrative unit with an independent government and set of laws to deal with its own affairs. For national and international purposes, these states are joined togther by a federal government—forming the United States.

...A region of the United States that has its own government and is part of the confederacy, but one not yet admitted to statehood.

Trafficking
The transporting and trade in humans for economic gain using force or deception.

Triangular trade
System by which ships departed Europe with goods to trade in Africa, took on board enslaved Africans, carried them to the Americas, and returned to Europe laden with goods from slave-worked plantations.

Underground Railroad
Support network established in the United States in the mid-19th century to help enslaved people escape from the slave states of the South to free states or Canada.

Unionist
A supporter of the Union, or United States government, in the Civil War, against attempted secession by the Confederate Southern states.

Voodoo
Form of religion and ritual combining traditional African beliefs with elements of Catholicism.

West Indies
The islands of the Caribbean, so-called because in 1492 Christopher Columbus, arriving there, thought he had reached Asia.

GLOSSARY

INDEX

191

The publisher would like to thank the following for their kind permission to reproduce their photographs: (Key: a-above; b-below/bottom; c-center; l-left; r-right; t-top)
Abbreviations:
AA - The Art Archive; AKG - akg-images; Alamy - Alamy Images; BAL - The Bridgeman Art Library; DK - DK Images; Getty - Getty Images; GC - The Granger Collection; LoC - Library of Congress Library, Washington, DC; MEPL - Mary Evans Picture Library

1 GC, New York. 2-3 Getty: Hulton Archive/C.Seaver Jr. 4-5 GC, New York: (l/6). 6 AA: (l/2). Corbis: Bettmann (l/4). Getty: Hulton Archive (l/3). GC, New York (l/5). Photoshot: AISA/World Illustrated (l/1). 8-9 Corbis: Sygma/Alberto Pizzoli. 10 AKG: Erich Lessing (bc). Alamy: The London Art Archive (tl). 11 Alamy: North Wind Picture Archives (tl). AA: Museo Provincial de Bellas Artes, Salamanca/Dagli Orti (ca); Palenque Site Museum, Chiapas/Gianni Dagli Orti (tr). iStockphoto.com: Cat London (b). 12 AKG: Hervé Champollion (br). Corbis: Zefa/Janicek Ladislav (tr). 12-13 AA: Archaeological Museum, Merida/Alfredo Dagli Orti (c). 13 AA: Bardo Museum, Tunis/Dagli Orti (br). The Kobal Collection: Universal/Bryna (tr). Photoshot: UPPA (tl). 14-15 AA: Bardo Museum, Tunis/Dagli Orti. 16 Alamy: MEPL (bc); The London Art Archive (tr); The Print Collector (br). Werner Forman Archive: National Museum, Copenhagen (bl). 17 AKG: Cameraphoto (br). Alamy: MEPL (bl). Getty: Victoria & Albert Museum, London (tl). AA: Antenna Gallery, Dakar/Dagli Orti (tr). iStockphoto.com: Bernhard Ertl (cl). 18-19 Still Pictures: Frans Lemmens (b). 19 Corbis: Bettmann (ca). Photoshot: AISA/World Illustrated (clb). 20-21 GC, New York. 22 AA: Museo de Arte Antiga, Lisbon/Dagli Orti (tl). 23 Alamy: The London Art Archive (tr). DK: Courtesy of the National Maritime Museum, London/James Stevenson and Tina Chambers (t, cl). LoC: L. Prang & Co. (c). 24 DK: The British Museum, London (c). 25 AKG: Biblioteca Colombina, Seville (cb); Staatsbibliothek Preußischer Kulturbesitz, Berlin (tl). DK: Courtesy of the Albuquerque Museum of Art and History, New Mexico/Francesca Yorke (tl). GC, New York: (cl). 26-27 AA: New York Public Library/Harper Collins Publishers. 28 Alamy: The London Art Archive (clb). 29 Alamy: North Wind Picture Archives (cr); photow.com (bc); The Print Collector (cl). AA: Lord Methuen (tl). 30-31 Alamy: North Wind Picture Archives (tl). 32 Alamy: Robert Estall Photo Agency (tl); MEPL (br). 33 Corbis: Stapleton Collection (l). Hannes Grobe: iStockphoto.com: Jan Kranendonk (tr). 34 Corbis: The Gallery Collection (bl). 35 Alamy: MEPL (tr); North Wind Picture Archives (clb); Alex Scheif (c). The National Archives: (co268-1-5) (br). 36 AA: The British Museum, London/Eileen Tweedy (br). BAL: British Library, London (t). 37 Alamy: North Wind Picture Archives (br). BAL: Ferens Art Gallery, Hull City Museums and Art Galleries (cr). DK: Courtesy of the Charlestown Shipwreck and Heritage Centre, Cornwall/Alex Wilson (tl/Tobacco). National Maritime Museum, London: (E5700) (b). 39 Alamy: The Print Collector (cra). BAL: Bristol City Museum and Art Gallery (bc). 40 Alamy: Danita Delimont (bl). AA: Bibliothèque des Arts Décoratifs, Paris/Dagli Orti (tl). BAL: Private Collection (cl). 40-41 BAL: Private Collection/Photo Christie's Images (b). 41 Alamy: Lebrecht Music and Arts Photo Library (tl); David Lyons (tr). 42-43 Corbis. 44 AKG: (t). iStockphoto.com: Danny Smythe (bl). 45 AA: Biblioteca Nazionale Marciana, Venice/Dagli Orti (br). BAL: Private Collection/Michael Graham-Stewart. DK: The Wallace Collection, London (tr). 46-47 BAL: Private Collection/Michael Graham-Stewart. 48 MEPL. 49 LoC: (bl). 50-51 BAL: Private Collection/Michael Graham-Stewart. 52 BAL: Private Collection (l); Stapleton Collection (tl). MEPL: (br). 53 AKG: (b). Alamy: MEPL (tr). DK: Wilberforce House, Hull City Council (tl). Photolibrary: Japan Travel Bureau (cl). 54 Getty: Kean Collection (tr). GC, New York: (cl). 54-55 AA: Eileen Tweedy (b). 55 Alamy: MEPL (tl). Corbis: (cra). DK: Wilberforce House Museum, Hull City Council (cl). 56-57 AA: Biblioteca Nazionale Marciana, Venice/Dagli Orti. 58 Corbis: Bettmann (br). DK: Wilberforce House Museum, Hull City Council (l). 59 AA: Private Collection/Marc Charmet (t). GC, New York: (cr, bl). 60-61 GC, New York. 62 Corbis: Bettmann (cra). DK: Courtesy of the National Maritime Museum, London/Tina Chambers (t). LoC: S.W. Fores (t). 63 AA: (cr). GC, New York: (t). 64-65 BAL: British Library, London. 66 BAL: American Antiquarian Society, Worcester, Massachusetts (t). Corbis: (bl). Bettmann (br). 67 Corbis: Bettmann (bl); Historical Picture Archive (br). GC, New York: (t). 68-69 AKG: Archiv für Kunst & Geschichte, Berlin. 70 AA: Bibliothèque des Arts Décoratifs, Paris/Dagli Orti (cr). Getty: Bibliothèque Nationale, Paris/BAL (br). GC, New York: (t). 72 AISA - Archivo Iconográfico S. A., Barcelona: (c). Alamy: The Print Collector (tr). BAL: Bibliothèque Nationale, Paris/Archives Charmet (b). 73 Alamy: North Wind Picture Archives (cr); The Print Collector (br). DK: Courtesy of the Natural History Museum, London/Harry Taylor (cra). MEPL: (br). 74 AKG: (t). 75 Alamy: North Wind Picture Archives (tr); Pictorial Press Ltd (cl). DK: Judith Miller/Bonhams (br). Getty: Bibliothèque Nationale, Paris/BAL (tr). 76-77 Getty: Bibliothèque Nationale, Paris/BAL. 78 BAL: Massachusetts Historical Society, Boston, MA (cla). GC, New York: (tl). 78-79 Getty: BAL (b). 79 AKG: Archiv für Kunst & Geschichte, Berlin (cla). Alamy: Ambient Images, Inc. GC, New York: (cr). 80 Alamy: North Wind Picture Archives (tr). BAL: Private Collection/Michael Graham-Stewart (r). 81 DK: Wilberforce House, Hull City Council (cl, clb). Getty: MPI (crb). LoC: (tr). 82-83 Getty: Biblioteca Nacional, Rio de Janeiro/Bridgeman Art Library. 84 Alamy: North Wind Picture Archives (tl, bl, crb). 85 Alamy: MEPL (tl). Corbis: (b). Getty: Hulton Archive (cra). 86 Alamy: North Wind Picture Archives (bl). BAL: Private Collection/Michael Graham-Stewart (t). GC, New York: (br). 87 Alamy: Robert Harding Picture Library Ltd (t). Getty: Private Collection/BAL (bl). 88 Alamy: Visual Arts Library, London (bl). 89 Alamy: The Print Collector (bl). Corbis: Bettmann (tr). Getty: Popperfoto (clb); Ian Waldie (crb). 90 GC, New York: (tl). 90-91 GC, New York: (b). 91 Alamy: North Wind Picture Archives (br). GC, New York: (cla). LoC: William A. Stephens (cl). 92-93 SuperStock. 94 Alamy: North Wind Picture Archives (t). Corbis: Bettmann (crb). MEPL: (bc). 95 BAL: Private Collection/Michael Graham-Stewart (tc). Getty: MPI (c). GC, New York: (bc). 96-97 Alamy: North Wind Picture Archives. 98 Courtesy of Cornell University, Ithaca, NY: (tr). DK: The Museum of London/John Chase (cl). Getty: Bibliothèque des Arts Decoratifs, Paris/BAL (br). Courtesy of the Library of Virginia, Richmond: (cl). 99 Alamy: North Wind Picture Archives (l). BAL: Royal Albert Memorial Museum, Exeter (crb). GC, New York: (tr). 100 Getty: Otto Herschan (b). GC, New York: (tr). Courtesy of the

Library of Virginia, Richmond: (cl). 101 BAL: Private Collection/The Bloomsbury Workshop, London (tl). GC, New York: (tr, br, cl). 102-103 GC, New York. 104 Getty: Hulton Archive (b). GC, New York: (tl). 105 Alamy: North Wind Picture Archives (tl). Corbis: Ken O'Brien Collection (br). Getty: Time Life Pictures (tr). GC, New York: (cl). 106 Corbis: Private Collection/Look and Learn (tl). DK: Courtesy of the Powell-Cotton Museum, Kent/Ray Moller (bc). GC, New York: (cl). 107 Corbis: Bettmann (tl); Bob Sacha (b). 108-109 AA: Musée Carnavalet, Paris/Dagli Orti. 110 Alamy: The London Art Archive (cl); North Wind Picture Archives (br). 110-111 Alamy: North Wind Picture Archives (t). MEPL: (tr). AA: British Museum, London (br). BAL: Musée de la Ville de Paris/Lauros/Giraudon (bl). 112 Corbis: Bettmann (tl, bl). 113 Alamy: North Wind Picture Archives (tr). AA: Laurie Platt Winfrey (tl). Colonial Williamsburg Foundation, VA: (cr). Photolibrary: North Wind Picture Archives (cl). 114 Corbis: Bettmann (t). 115 DK: Courtesy of the National Constitution Center/Demetrio Carrasco (b). GC, New York: (tc, bl). 116-117 Corbis: Bettmann. 118 BAL: British Library, London (tl). The Royal Cornwall Museum: © Royal Institution of Cornwall (b). 119 Alamy: MEPL (clb); Nic Hamilton Photographic (crb). BAL: National Portrait Gallery, London (bc). V&A: (t). 120 BAL: Wilberforce House, Hull City Museums and Art Galleries (clb). Corbis: Angelo Hornak (c). GC, New York: (tr). 121 AA: (tl, bc). BAL: National Portrait Gallery, London (c). Getty: Private Collection/BAL (tr). 122-123 Getty: Private Collection/BAL. 124 Corbis: Austrian Archives (t). 125 AA: Museo Naval, Madrid/Dagli Orti (c). BAL: Private Collection (cla). GC, New York: (tl). The Kobal Collection: Dreamworks LLC (tr). 126 DK: The British Museum, London/Chas Howson (c). Getty: Hulton Archive (tl). 126-127 BAL: Royal Geographical Society, London (b). 127 BAL: LoC (c). Corbis: Bettmann (tr). LoC: (tl). 128-129 Corbis. 130 AKG: (bl). AA: Musée Carnavalet, Paris/Dagli Orti (tr). 131 Alamy: The London Art Archive (cr). BAL: Private Collection/Michael Graham-Stewart (c). Getty: Bibliothèque Nationale, Paris/BAL (tl); Roger Viollet Collection (tr). Courtesy of the Library of Virginia, Richmond: (br). 132-133 Corbis: Bettmann. 134 Alamy: Lee Karen Stow (l). GC, New York: (crb). 135 Alamy: Jon Arnold Images Ltd (tr). AA: (cla, bl). BAL: Wilberforce House, Hull City Museums and Art Galleries (tl). 136 GC, New York: (cl). 136-137 GC, New York: (t). 137 Corbis: Burstein Collection (cr); Profiles in History (bl). GC, New York: (tr). 138 Alamy: North Wind Picture Archives (cb). GC, New York: (tl). iStockphoto.com: Clayton Hansen (t). 139 Getty: Private Collection/BAL (tr). GC, New York: (tl). LoC: (tl). 140-141 GC, New York. 142 Alamy: The London Art Archive (bc). BAL: Massachusetts Historical Society, Boston, MA (bl). LoC: (br). 143 Getty: Hulton Archive (br). GC, New York: (t, bc, bl). 144-145 AA: American Antiquarian Society, Worcester, Massachusetts (tr). Corbis: Bettmann (bl). 147 Courtesy of Cornell University, Ithaca, NY: (tl). GC, New York: (tc, bl, br, cra). 148-149 GC, New York. 150 BAL: Private Collection/Photo Christie's Images (t). GC, New York: (bc). 151 Alamy: North Wind Picture Archives (cl); Stock Montage, Inc. (cra). Corbis: Bettmann (tl); Louie Psihoyos (crb). Getty: National Geographic/Jerry Pinkney (bl). 152 Corbis: Bettmann (tr). GC, New York: (cl, br, tl). 153 Alamy: MEPL (crb); North Wind Picture Archives (t). GC, New York: (bl). 154 DK: Courtesy of the Gettysburg National Military Park, PA/Dave King (c). GC, New York: (tr, br). 155 GC, New York: (tl, tr). LoC: (bl). 156-157 Corbis: Brooklyn Museum. 158 Corbis: Walter Bibikow (t). LoC: (bl). 158-159 AA: Culver Pictures (t). 159 Alamy: Old Paper Studios (tr); Don Smetzer (tl). Corbis: Bettmann (cr). 160 iStockphoto.com: Duncan Walker (cl, bl). 161 GC, New York: (bl). LoC: (c, bl); Philp & Solomons (tr). 162 Getty: Stock Montage (br). GC, New York: (tr, tl, clb). LoC: (bl). 163 BAL: Vermont Historical Society, VT (tc). GC, New York. 166 Corbis: Bettmann (crb). GC, New York: (tl). The US National Archives and Records Administration: (bl). 167 Alamy: North Wind Picture Archives (br). BAL: Chicago History Museum (t). LoC: (clb). 168-169 Alamy: North Wind Picture Archives. 170 BAL: Museo Nacional de Bellas Artes, Havana (t). GC, New York: (clb). 171 Alamy: North Wind Picture Archives (tl). AA: Museo Historico Nacional, Rio de Janeiro/Gianni Dagli Orti (bl). GC, New York: (tl). 172-173 Corbis: Louie Psihoyos. 174 Alamy: North Wind Picture Archives (tl); The Print Collector (cl). 174-175 GC, New York: (bc). 175 GC, New York: (tl, tr). LoC: Daniel Murray Collection (t). 176 Getty: Henry Guttmann (tl). LoC: (cla); Brady-Handy Photograph Collection (t). 177 Corbis: Bettmann (t). GC, New York: (cb, bl). 178 Getty: Time Life Pictures/Francis Miller (t). LoC: George Grantham Bain Collection (clb). 179 Corbis: Bettmann (tl); EPA/Tannen Maury (c); Sygma/J.P. Laffont (br). Getty: Express/William Lovelace (clb); Time Life Pictures/Don Cravens (tl). 180 The Kobal Collection: Epic (bl); Warner Bros TV/David L. Wolper Productions (br). Rex Features: Everett Collection (bc). 181 Alamy: Tom Uhlman (t). Corbis: EPA/Pierre Holtz (bc); Reuters/Juda Ngwenya (br). 182-183 The Kobal Collection: Warner Bros TV/David L. Wolper Productions. 184 Corbis: Liaison/Vincent Boon (bl); Shaul Schwarz (br). Still Pictures: Ron Giling (tl). 185 Getty: Matt Cardy (br). Rex Features: Dave Gatley (clb). Still Pictures: Mark Edwards (t). 186-187 Corbis: Macduff Everton

Jacket images: Front: Alamy Images: Bill Bachmann ftl (jugs); North Wind Picture Archives fbl; PhotoSpin, Inc. c (background); The Print Collector tc; Helene Rogers tl (asiatic slaves). The Art Archive: fclb. The Bridgeman Art Library: Collection of the New-York Historical Society, USA fcrb, ftr (ship layout). Corbis: Bettmann/Timothy H. O'Sullivan c; Historical Picture Archive fcra; Tugela Ridley/Epa fbr. Getty Images: Liaison/Vincent Boon br (carpet); Lightfoot/Hulton Archive bc. The Granger Collection, New York: bl (douglass), fcla. Panos Pictures: G. M. B. Akash bc (sewing); Giacomo Pirozzi br. Still Pictures: Mark Edwards br (forest). Back: Corbis: David H. Wells. Spine: Alamy Images: PhotoSpin, Inc. t (background). Corbis: Bettmann/Timothy H. O'Sullivan

All other images © Dorling Kindersley. For further information see: www.dkimages.com
Thanks to Marion Dent for proofreading, Jackie Brind for indexing, and Shaila Brown for editorial help. The publisher wishes to acknowledge the following: page 183 From "Malcolm X Speaks" by Malcolm X, published by Secker & Warburg, reprinted by permission of The Random House Group Ltd., and copyright © 1965, 1989 by Betty Shabazz and Pathfinder Press, reprinted by permission; page 183 Kwame Kwei-Armah for permission to include his quote. Every effort has been made to contact the rights owners in each case but the publisher would welcome information on any omissions.

CREDITS AND ACKNOWLEDGMENTS